THE FUNDAMENTALS OF
Judo

THE FUNDAMENTALS OF
Judo

Ray Stevens and Edward Semple

THE CROWOOD PRESS

First published in 2012 by
The Crowood Press Ltd
Ramsbury, Marlborough
Wiltshire SN8 2HR

www.crowood.com

British Library Cataloguing-in-Publication Data
A catalogue record for this book is available from the British Library.

ISBN 978 1 84797 414 3

Typeset by Phoenix Typesetting, Auldgirth, Dumfriesshire

Printed and bound in Signapore by Craft Print International Ltd

CONTENTS

DEDICATION

This book is dedicated to Elvis Gordon. May you rest in peace my friend.

ACKNOWLEDGEMENTS

The authors extend their sincere thanks to Hilary Walker who drew the illustrations to this book and proof read the text. Her input has simply been invaluable. Hilary's website is a must for anyone who likes the illustrations in this book www.hilarywalker.co.uk. Hilary was given permission to observe and photograph a black belt training session at the Kodokan Dojo in Tokyo, Japan. The images she took away from that visit inspired the illustrations in this book. Patrick Jackson took the photos for the book and the authors would like to thank him for his incredible patience and support.

Photographs © Patrick Jackson
www.patrickjacksonimages.com

Illustrations © Hilary Walker
Illustrations by Hilary Walker are available for purchase as prints from
www.hilarywalker.co.uk

FOREWORD

Among British judoka Ray Stevens stands out as one of those who have done more than most to make the sport of judo better known and accessible to a wide audience. His achievements in judo are well known: an Olympic Silver Medallist who has trained and competed successfully in many parts of the world, he is now Vice-Chairman of the London Area.

Ray's passion for judo started at a young age when his focus and determination soon became apparent. Having had the privilege of observing his career over many years, I was delighted to learn that he had decided to present his skills, experience and judo insights in a new book. Ray is a popular and accomplished teacher and his fresh and engaging style, accompanied by his sound techniques, will appeal to beginners and the more experienced practitioner alike.

Judo is a sport that never stands still: as well as re-interpreting ideas from the past, it is always evolving, and I believe that this book will convey its fascination, variety and excitement to a new generation of readers.

Tony Sweeney, 9th Dan

CHAPTER I

THE HISTORY AND DEVELOPMENT OF JUDO

Judo was developed from the Japanese martial art ju-jitsu at the turn of the twentieth century by Jigaro Kano. It is important, therefore, that any historical record of judo recognizes the essential role ju-jitsu played in the development of judo. Although both judo and ju-jitsu come from Japan, the origin of the techniques that define them both probably came from elsewhere.

Nearly all ancient cultures had some form of grappling or unarmed fighting but it was really the Greeks who had the first documented system of unarmed combat. From ancient Greece came Alexander the Great, who had conquered most of the world around 300 years before the birth of Christ, and he first introduced wrestling to India. Many believe that it was the technical changes made to wrestling in India around this time that led to the birth of ju-jitsu. There is certainly a strong similarity between the pinning and throwing techniques of ju-jitsu and those of Greco-Roman wrestling.

Most historians agree that the first documented system of unarmed combat to reach China came from India, along with Buddhism. How much influence Chinese culture had on Japan is impossible to say but clearly the early fighting techniques that came from India and that led to the development of kung fu must have had an influence on Japan. Although Japan at times has tried to limit its contact with the outside world, there is a rich history of trade and war between Japan and China. The Japanese principles and beliefs that were central to the development of sumo and ju-jitsu must have been influenced by events in China. Incredibly, many of these ancient principles and beliefs underpin judo practice today.

Many of the myths surrounding the creation of Japan talk of gods such as Bishman, the God of War, locked in unarmed combat with evil demons from the Underworld, such as Mikaboshi, fighting for power and supremacy. These early descriptions are often regarded as the first descriptions of sumo. Sumo certainly started as a form o wrestling designed to help warriors train for battle and was very different from the sumo seen on television today. There would have been a much greater range of techniques including kicks, punches, throws and locks. Sumo is widely regarded as an important influence in the development of ju-jitsu. It is from this early sumo that the origin of many of ju-jitsu's grappling techniques can be traced.

What is clear is that over hundreds of years the Japanese developed and constantly refined a very sophisticated fighting system known as ju-jitsu. Much of how ju-jitsu developed inevitably reflects how Japan developed and changed as a country. This link between Japanese society and ju-jitsu is a central and important theme in the formation and development of judo. These stories and myths that surround the development of ju-jitsu and then judo are an important part of Japanese history. They reflect the social changes Japan was going through at that particular time. These two arts did not simply spring into existence: they evolved and developed because of very important social issues and principles in Japanese society. This is important because many of these issues and principles still shape and govern the sport of judo today. It is only by looking back at the history and development of ju-jitsu and Japan that we can understand the principles and beliefs that were so important to Jigaro Kano and the development of judo.

Ju-Jitsu

Early Japanese history is defined by conflict and war. From the beginning of records right through to and including the Middle Ages there was very little so cial stability. Japan was ruled by warlords who constantly fell in and out of alliances. War between these differing warlords was common and the skills of a good soldier (samurai) were much in demand. The chief skills of the samurai at this time were archery, riding and sword fighting.

Ju-jitsu techniques were your last option on the battlefield when you had no weapon or horse and you were up close to the enemy. In essence, ju-jitsu was unarmed combat. Sword fighting was the primary discipline of the warrior, but ju-jitsu would have been seen as a natural extension of sword fighting because grappling was a natural extension of what you had to do when swords met and you were up close to your enemy. Also, not all fights took place on the battlefield; many fights were in limited spaces such as in crowded marketplaces or narrow corridors where the use of a sword was not as effective. There were also certain social situations where the carrying of a sword was forbidden.

Essentially, ju-jitsu was technically comprised of strikes (kicks and punches), throws, strangles and locks. These techniques could be used to kill, maim or restrain, depending on the situation. Although the primary purpose was to train the warrior in hand-to-hand fighting, ju-jitsu would also have included the use of short weapons such as the knife. The knife in particular was a popular weapon of choice and seen as an ideal weapon for close-quarter fighting. This close-quarter fighting was what ju-jitsu was designed for, so ju-jitsu would have employed attacks and defences both with and against small weapons. Given the constant state of war between the rival warlords, these ju-jitsu skills were constantly refined and developed through generation after generation of samurai, and they developed over hundreds of years of constant war and conflict to a level of brutal effectiveness. Different samurai would have specialized in different ju-jitsu techniques depending on the role given to them by their warlord, resulting in the rise of the ninja, experts in stealth, assignation and murder.

While war defined the early development of ju-jitsu, it was ironically peace that defined the later development of ju-jitsu and eventually led to the birth of judo. After a long series of wars, Japan was unified under one ruling clan in 1603. To keep peace and stability a system of social control was introduced, which was so effective that there was peace for the next 250 years. This system of control worked because it effectively governed just about every aspect of Japanese life including the teaching and practice of ju-jitsu.

Society was divided into distinct groups, each governed by strict laws and regulations. The ruling elite were the samurai who enjoyed privileges the lower social groups, such as the peasants, did not. The samurai were allowed to carry a sword and had the right to kill anybody of another social group if they thought it necessary. However, there was also a clear hierarchy within the samurai group: the lower-ranked samurai were foot soldiers or clerks while the higher-ranked samurai were landed aristocrats or bureaucrats. Every aspect of their lives would have been governed by the laws and regulations that had been imposed upon Japanese society and, importantly, this would have included their education. The samurai were the only social group allowed to carry and use weapons so only they would have had to learn skills such as sword

fighting and ju-jitsu. The other social groups such as the peasants or farmers would have had their own fighting techniques, in this case karate. Karate means 'empty hand', a reflection of the fact that this social group was not allowed to carry weapons. The weapons used in karate go back to the farming implements that the peasants/farmers were allowed to use for working on the land. Karate students today still train with weapons such as the bo, a long wooden staff, and the kama, a vicious cutting weapon based upon the sickle. This distinction is very important because the development of ju-jitsu and then judo was based upon the beliefs and principles of the samurai, the warrior class of Japanese society and, as such, a unique social group within that society.

A samurai's education was compulsory. He would have had to learn and train regularly in different fighting skills such as the sword and ju-jitsu. However, a samurai was expected to be much more than just a warrior: he would have been expected to study other subjects such as literature and art. A samurai was expected to be highly skilled and educated. The training hall in which the samurai learnt these skills was the dojo, which was seen as a sacred place of learning. Here they learnt to develop the physical, mental and spiritual skills and the values essential to their role in Japanese society. The education the samurai received in the dojo was a well-rounded one and was as much about the development of the individual as the development of a skilled fighter. This would later be a central and guiding principle in the development of judo as well. Even in judo today we refer to the place we train in as the dojo. In judo classes all over the world the dojo is still seen as a special place of learning and education.

As this was now a period of social stability and peace, ju-jitsu began to change. This long period of peace meant that ju-jitsu was no longer needed on the battlefield and so was now primarily a form of unarmed combat taught and practised in the dojo. Ju-jitsu was the fighting art of the ruling elite. Still brutal and effective, it was also vital that the practice of ju-jitsu reflected the complex code of honour and etiquette so important to the Japanese ruling class of the time. As a result, the practice of ju-jitsu became much more formal and there was a strict code of conduct for all samurai when they learnt and practised ju-jitsu in the dojo. This code of conduct is still a fundamental part of modern judo practice. The formal bow to your opponent before you engage in combat is still as important in judo today as it was back then to the samurai warrior. The samurai code of respect, humility and decorum is still fundamental to the proper practice of judo.

This shift in ju-jitsu from battlefield to dojo also changed the martial art technically. The fighting techniques of ju-jitsu had primarily been designed for the chaos of the battlefield and an opponent dressed in armour. However, ju-jitsu was now primarily practised in a dojo, usually on mats, in bare feet against an opponent who wore loose-fitting clothes of cloth, and the fight was usually one on one. Ju-jitsu still technically consisted of strikes, strangles, locks, throws and the use of small weapons but the more controlled environment of the dojo allowed the development of a much greater range of techniques. Each dojo would have taught the same set of basic skills but each would also have favoured and emphasized certain techniques more than others. Which techniques were given the most importance depended entirely on what the individual master, who was the principle instructor at the dojo, thought were the most effective and important. This led to a proliferation of what is called different 'styles' of ju-jitsu. This distinction still exists today, with different styles being practised all over the world. Usually the style of ju-jitsu taught at a specific dojo stayed within the family, with the master passing both his role and style of ju-jitsu on to his son.

The master of each dojo would have to have been a skilled expert and able to put into practice what he taught. At any time, a master from another dojo could challenge him or any of his students to a fight, and students from each of the different dojos would have regularly fought one another in contests. There was also a well-known practice where samurai warriors would meet at certain known crossroads at night and take on anybody who wanted to fight. These fights had no rules: you won or you lost. It is interesting to note that these fights were similar in style to that of modern cage fighting. Each samurai warrior would have brought a wide range of technical fighting skills to the contest but each fighter would have had particular technical fighting skills that they specialized in. Some would have been better strikers (punches and kicks), others would have been better grapplers (locks, holds and throws) and some would have been better fighting on the ground than in the stand-up position. Each fighter would have tried to dominate the fight with his strengths and thereby expose the weaknesses of his opponent.

While each dojo may have taught different styles of ju-jitsu, all would have followed the ethical code of the samurai warrior, called budo or bushido, which defined what it meant to be a samurai warrior. The manner in which a samurai lived and died was very important. The beliefs and practices of Zen Buddhism were central to the samurai approach to life. Simplicity and a life free from the fear of death were core principles to being a good samurai. This is beautifully illustrated in the life of the samurai warrior Miyamoto Musashi, who lived in the early 1600s. Miyamoto Musashi believed that there was only one goal, victory, and that there was no other point to combat. He was a master swordsman and travelled Japan challenging different masters from all over the country to fight. He died at the age of sixty, undefeated. Not only was he an exceptional swordsman but, like all samurai, he was very well educated. Thanks to his samurai education, he was not only a skilled fighter but also an accomplished painter, poet and sculptor. He believed that hard work, simplicity and discipline were essential if you were to learn and that only a life of loyalty, duty and honour was worth living. Only a life well lived prepared you for death. It is only when you understand the importance of these values to the Japanese samurai that you can comprehend how vital etiquette, manners and honour were to the proper practice of ju-jitsu. Much of the later success of judo both in Japan and abroad was due to the fact that judo has tried to retain many of these values and practices.

Gradually Japanese society began to change: the four-class system declined and was eventually abolished. This was particularly hard for the samurai warriors because they no longer enjoyed the special status and privileges that had been their preserve for so long. Japan was no longer so insular and wanted more international trade. To do so, Japan began to modernize and one of the key areas to change fundamentally was the Japanese education system. The Japanese ruling elite still believed in the values and principles that defined what it was to be a samurai, but now the general belief was that all Japanese men and women should follow the ethical code of the samurai warrior. The values and principles of budo or bushido should not just be for one particular section of Japanese society but for the whole of Japan. This would result in Japan becoming stronger as a country and therefore more competitive and successful on the international stage.

It was these changes in the education system that gave Jigaro Kano, the founder of judo, the opportunity to develop and promote judo. He used the core values and practices of ju-jitsu as the fundamental basis of judo because these were the very qualities that he wanted to develop and promote in the young men and women of Japan. Jigaro Kano represented everything that was new about Japan and how the country was changing. He developed judo as a way to teach, promote and spread the values and principles of budo or bushido to all social classes both in Japan and abroad.

Jigaro Kano

Jigaro Kano is the founding father of judo. It was his vision to take ju-jitsu and remould it into a sport that would be better suited to a more modern Japanese society. In doing so he created something that in a little more than 100 years has evolved from a small personal project in a small hall to an international sport that has a rich Olympic history – an incredible journey by any standards.

Jigaro Kano was born in 1860 in the city of Kobe. His father worked in Tokyo for the government and had strong links with both the Imperial household and the government. The Kano family was part of Japan's ruling class, and the importance of these social connections to Jigaro Kano when he later wanted to promote judo both in Japan and abroad cannot be underestimated.

In 1870, Jigaro Kano's mother died when he was just ten years old. The young Jigaro therefore went to live with his father in Tokyo where he received a first-class education. He was very bright and at the age of fifteen he was enrolled at the foreign language school in Tokyo. Jigaro Kano's ability in foreign languages was exceptional and he learnt to write fluently in English. These skills would be important when he later started to promote judo outside Japan and work towards getting judo accepted into the Olympic Games.

In 1877, aged eighteen, Jigaro Kano went to Tokyo University to study political science, economics and education for four years . His studies there left him with a passion for education that would define the rest of his life. He believed that a good education was the foundation stone to a well-balanced and successful society. His belief in the importance of education would have been a popular and widely held view in Japan at this time. Japan for the first time in several hundred years was looking outwards to other countries and now wanted to compete on the world stage and trade with countries such as Britain, America and Russia. A good education system was vital if Japan was to adapt to this new, competitive world. Japan wanted to modernize her education system and it was well-educated men such as Jigaro Kano who would help define and shape this. Jigaro Kano, with his founding of judo, was very much in the right place at the right time.

Jigaro Kano considered education to have essentially three main components:

- Knowledge, meaning the technical detail a student needed to learn for a subject.
- Ethics, meaning the moral values a student should learn.
- Health and fitness, meaning the training of the body as well as areas such as diet and hygiene.

This definition of what a good education should comprise would have been very much in tune with Japanese thinking. The Japanese had always put great value in knowledge and the application of sound technical principles. This can be seen throughout history in Japanese architecture and art, which are usually exquisite in detail. The education of the samurai had focused on an honourable life, and the value of virtues such as honesty and simplicity. These were values that the ruling class of Japan still held dear in principle and would have wanted to continue as the focus of any new education system. Health and fitness were vital components to being a productive member of Japanese society. The education of the samurai had encompassed both mind and body and both were important in the individual's education and development. Clean, healthy living was a prerequisite to creating the right environment for learning and personal development. It is no accident that the structure of judo in Japan was built upon these guiding principles.

When Jigaro Kano went to study at Tokyo University he also began studying ju-jitsu. Quite why he decided to take up ju-jitsu at this time is somewhat of a mystery. There are stories that he started to learn ju-jitsu because he was being bullied at school and wanted to learn how to defend himself. I am not so sure this is correct. Jigaro Kano was now eighteen years old and had just left school; he was embarking on what was a new chapter in his life. Problems at school, if they did exist, would have been left behind. This was a new beginning and I think it much more likely that Jigaro Kano, like any young man, wanted to try new and different things. Ju-jitsu was part of Japanese history and the educated samurai warrior class. It is much more likely that it was these influences that first attracted him to ju-jitsu.

Records are contradictory as to the style of ju-jitsu Jigaro Kano may have learnt and whom he learnt his ju-jitsu from; what is clear is that he studied ju-jitsu for only four years. He left Tokyo University in 1882 at the age of twenty-two and accepted a teaching job at the Peers school. The Peers school was held in very high regard and Jigaro Kano would have taught the children of the most powerful and influential families in Japan. The social connections he made here, coupled with those of his family, were to be very important to the later success of judo.

When he accepted his new teaching post, he set up his own ju-jitsu school and called his style of ju-jitsu, judo. His dojo was called the Kodokan, had nine students and an area of just 22sq m (26sq yd) to train in. This was an extraordinary step for the young and inexperienced Jigaro Kano to take and it tells us much about his confidence and ability to understand how Japan was changing. The masters who taught ju-jitsu at this time quite literally devoted their lives to their own style of ju-jitsu. Their technical knowledge and skill were acquired over decades, not months and years. After just four years of study, Jigaro Kano could not have had the technical skills or knowledge to regard himself as a particularly skilled fighter or gifted teacher of ju-jitsu. He set up the Kodokan and started to teach judo because he wanted to take ju-jitsu in a different direction. His vision was to marry the practice of ju-jitsu with his other great passion in life, education. At the Kodokan there was not only judo practice but also lectures on a wide range of topics such as physiology, diet and hygiene. The Kodokan was based upon the two defining themes of Jigaro Kano's life: education and the practice of judo.

Judo

Technically, Jigaro Kano struggled at first to convince anyone that judo was really any different from any other style of ju-jitsu in Japan. Indeed, the technical differences between ju-jitsu and judo would have been very small in the beginning. The system of techniques that helped define judo evolved over time. It was not until 1887 that the core techniques of judo could be defined in what we would today regard as some kind of syllabus. After establishing the Kodokan dojo, Jigaro Kano kept on developing and refining the technical elements of judo, a process that in many ways has never stopped. For judo is not a fixed set of skills and even today the technical side of judo is constantly changing and developing.

To Jigaro Kano sport was a vital part of a proper physical education and therefore a central component to a well-balanced education. He may have struggled at first to separate ju-jitsu and judo technically but it is the greater emphasis that judo placed upon being a sport that separated ju-jitsu and judo right from the start. Judo had three principle objectives:

1. Combat.
2. Moral education.
3. Physical education.

The first two objectives are very similar to those of ju-jitsu, but not the third. The idea of transforming ju-jitsu into a sport was new and visionary and allowed judo to develop and grow with the social changes that Japan was going through at the turn of the twentieth century.

Jigaro Kano must have been profoundly influenced by what was happening in America and Europe at that time. Physical education and sport were undergoing huge changes and becoming ever more popular in the West. It would not be long before the Olympic movement began to take shape and launch so many different sports on to the international stage. In developing judo as a form of physical education and a competitive sport, Jigaro Kano would have used developments abroad as his model and inspiration. By taking ju-jitsu as his starting point, he developed a sport that was relevant to Japan, a sport that reflected important Japanese customs, values and beliefs. However, his approach was new and different and reflected how sport was developing abroad. This would be fundamental to the success of judo not only in Japan but all over the world.

To make judo into a sport, Jigaro Kano banned the more dangerous techniques in ju-jitsu. This meant that the practice of judo was relatively safe and a very effective form of exercise in developing and improving general levels of fitness. Judo allowed students to practice a sport they enjoyed and in the process get very fit and strong. Judo was and is a more limited form of ju-jitsu and these limitations make the practice of judo safer but importantly still preserve judo as an effective form of combat. These qualities can probably be most clearly seen in the practice of randori. Randori is essentially where students fight one another but under a strict set of rules, the rules that define judo as a sport. These fights were much safer than the no-rules contests of ju-jitsu but still very realistic. This meant that students of judo sustained far fewer injuries than those of ju-jitsu but still had the technical abilities to defend themselves.

Jigaro Kano established the Kodokan dojo at just the right time because Japan was ready for the formation and development of a sporting form of ju-jitsu. What he cannot have expected was that the rest of the world was also ready for a sporting form of ju-jitsu as well. The success and expansion of his Kodokan dojo mirror the success and expansion of judo at first in Japan and then abroad. The dojo grew from a 22sq m (26sq yd) training area in 1882, to 197sq m (236sq yd) in 1893, to 378sq m (452sq yd) in 1906 and to 933sq m (1,116sq yd) in 1934. In 1984, the Kodokan dojo was completely rebuilt with a fantastic training area, accommodation and a museum. What started as a small training area with nine students was within 100 years the centre for an international sport that was part of the Olympics.

There can be no doubt that the Olympic movement played a huge role in making judo the international sport it is today. In 1909, Japan was asked by Baron Pierre de Coubertin to join the Olympic movement. Jigaro Kano was chosen as Japan's representative on the International Olympic Committee and in 1911 the Japanese Amateur Athletic Association was founded and Jigaro Kano became the first President. These two organizations were the perfect platform from which to promote judo both at home and abroad. The first Japanese Judo Championships were held in 1930 and continue today. Interestingly, there were no weight categories in 1930. In 1951, the International Judo Federation was formed and the first World Judo Championships were held in 1956, with judo becoming an Olympic sport in 1964. However, women's judo was slower to establish itself both in Japan and abroad. The first Japanese Women's Judo Championships were not held until 1978 and it was not until 1987 that the World Judo Championships included both men and women. In 1992, women competed at the Olympics for the first time, twenty-eight years after judo became an Olympic sport.

Jigaro Kano's vision, social connections and drive propelled judo into the international sporting arena in a way that no other oriental martial art had ever achieved. An explosion in the popularity of martial arts films brought many different martial arts such as kung fu and aikido to the attention of the West, but these arts have not had the same success as judo in adapting the combat element of their art to the sporting arena. However, this has put pressure on judo to continue to evolve and change technically. Judo is no different from any other sport: to survive and grow, judo needs to be televised and appeal to the widest possible audience. The World Championships and the Olympics are now very important as a means of promoting judo as a sport to the world. In order to improve the appeal of judo as a spectator sport, the International Judo Federation (IJF) has continued to develop the stand-up or throwing elements of judo at the expense of many of the ground-fighting techniques. Now more and more fighters are restricted from fighting on the floor and forced to fight in the stand-up position in the false belief that this improves judo as a sport for the spectator. In my opinion, this is a mistake and a mistake that has come back to haunt judo with the ever-increasing popularity of Brazilian ju-jitsu.

Brazilian Ju-Jitsu

The Brazilian jiu-jitsu story is important and one that judo should learn from. In 1897, Mitsuyo Maeda started his judo training at the Kodokan dojo. His was a very special talent. In 1904, at the age of twenty-six and already with a 4th Dan black belt, Mitsuyo Maeda was offered the opportunity to travel to America to promote judo. However, his trip was not a success. The object of the visit was to put on a judo demonstration at the West Point Military Academy. The Americans did not understand the techniques, though, and in frustration one of the students challenged Mitsuyo Maeda to a fight. The student was a wrestling champion so he thought he had won the fight when he pinned Mitsuyo Maeda to the ground. Mitsuyo Maeda had no understanding of wrestling rules so he continued to fight until he had put his opponent in a joint lock and made him submit. So both fighters felt that they had won the fight and that their own fighting skills were therefore superior.

Mitsuyo Maeda stayed in America but instead of teaching judo he became a prizefighter, using his judo skills to make money. He accepted fights against anyone who wanted to take him on, usually against much bigger men because at 1.65m (5ft 5in) and 69.9kg (154lb) he was a relatively small man. He fought anyone, whatever their background or martial art; from boxers to wrestlers, from prizefighters to street fighters, Mitsuyo Maeda beat them all. He had over 2,000 fights and travelled all over North, Central and South America as well as Europe using his superb judo skills to dominate and beat his opponents. Interestingly, he challenged the then heavyweight boxing champion of the world Jack Johnson, who quite shrewdly

declined the fight. Importantly, it was Mitsuyo Maeda's technical skills on the ground that tended to give him the edge and allowed him to defeat opponents who were physically much larger than him. However, in truth Mitsuyo Maeda had simply taken his judo skills and reverted back to ju-jitsu. He was just like the samurai of old who met at the crossroads and fought anyone who wanted to fight. In fighting for money Mitsuyo Maeda had gone completely against the founding principles of Jigaro Kano and judo. Jigaro Kano established judo on three fundamental principles: combat, moral education and physical education. Mitsuyo Maeda had no interest in sport or education; just like the samurai of old, he fought simply to win. What is fascinating is that technically he could adjust his judo so quickly to the old style of ju-jitsu fighting. Judo had already come a long way as a sport but it was still a very effective form of combat and, as Mitsuyo Maeda proved, not so very different from the ju-jitsu that judo had developed from. This adjustment in fighting style could not be made by a judo player today. By continually watering down the importance of groundwork over the years, the combat element of judo today has been weakened.

In 1915, Mitsuyo Maeda settled in Brazil, a country he loved, and his fame as a fighter allowed him to set up and open his own successful dojo and teach. The Brazilian people loved him and came from all over the country to train with him. It was when a local politician, Gastão Gracie, asked Mitsuyo Maeda to teach his son Carlos that the magic really began and a fighting dynasty was created. The Gracie family took the fighting skills of Mitsuyo Maeda and spread them across Brazil. Just the same as in the old ju-jitsu schools of Japan, each school in Brazil would have favoured and emphasized certain techniques more than others. Which techniques were given the most importance depended entirely on what the principal instructor thought was most effective. Again, just like the old ju-jitsu schools of Japan, the head of each dojo in Brazil would have to have been highly skilled because at any time he could be challenged to fight. The students from each of the different dojos would regularly fight in contests and like the samurai of Japan these fights had few rules, if any – you simply won or lost. Just as in the old ju-jitsu schools of Japan, the head of each dojo would tend to pass on his knowledge and role to his son; thus the importance of generation after generation of the Gracie family to the development of Brazilian ju-jitsu.

It is this tradition of no-rules fighting and of fighting any opponent from another martial art that defines Brazilian ju-jitsu. Brazilian ju-jitsu evolved over a similar timescale to judo and became immensely popular in Brazil. However, Brazilian ju-jitsu did not just captivate Brazilian audiences but also captured the imagination of North American television audiences. It was the Gracie family who bought the Ultimate Fighting Championship to the USA in the early

1990s and it was American audiences who were dazzled by the skill and brilliance of the Gracie fighters. The Ultimate Fighting Championship is a no-rules contest in an octagonal ring where fighters from any martial art can compete and fight. The Brazilian ju-jitsu fighters were to dominate this arena, defeating fighters from boxing, karate, wrestling, muay thai, kick-boxing and a host of other martial arts. America woke up to the fact that Brazilian ju-jitsu had been developed and refined specifically to compete with fighters from any martial art. The octagonal ring was the ideal platform for Brazilian ju-jitsu fighters to show just how effective they were against those from other fighting arts. It was here in the brutal combat of the octagonal ring that America and the rest of the world woke up to the phenomenon of mixed martial arts, now considered to be the fastest-growing martial art and sport in the world today.

Until then, a fighter was usually defined by the martial art he or she competed in. Boxers competed against other boxers, judo players competed against other judo players; fighters only competed against fighters from the same discipline or martial art. Technically, a fighter therefore developed the skill set he or she needed to beat other fighters from the same martial art. The octagon ring changed all that overnight: now there was a huge range of different martial arts all competing in the same ring. Boxers fought wrestlers, striking arts fought grappling arts and therefore the skills a fighter needed to have to compete were now much more complex and broad. Today any mixed martial arts fighter knows that great stand-up skills are not enough on their own to make them an effective fighter. Without good stand-up and good ground-fighting skills, a mixed martial arts fighter is really going to struggle. Judo and the other martial arts of the world had focused in the previous fifty years almost exclusively on improving their stand-up fighting techniques. Brazilian ju-jitsu reminded everyone just how important it was to keep that balance of technical skills in both the stand-up and groundwork positions. The rest of the world had to re-evaluate the skills necessary to be a complete and effective fighter.

As judo has tried to cement a tradition and position as a sport, the combat element of the art has been weakened. More and more techniques have been made illegal and the rules have become more and more restrictive and complex. Essentially, judo is a form of ju-jitsu and the primary aim of ju-jitsu is combat. Jigaro Kano wanted judo to be safer than ju-jitsu because he wanted to reduce the number of injuries that students suffered in training. For Jigaro Kano there was a time for technical practice and a time for competition, and competition should always be effective and realistic. What is truly remarkable about Jigaro Kano is that he got the balance right from the beginning. The rules he defined, and then applied, and which were ultimately to define judo as a sport got the balance between sport and combat correct.

Judo as a sport flourished under the guidance of Jigaro Kano but also remained a very effective form of combat. The fact that Mitsuyo Maeda was such a successful prizefighter shows just how effective judo was as a form of combat. This in part was due to the fact that Jigaro Kano got the technical balance between stand-up and groundwork technically correct. He wanted to encourage and develop a strong stand-up component to judo but not at the expense of a strong set of groundwork skills. Technical changes in judo by the International Judo Federation (IJF) since Jigaro Kano's death are well intentioned but ultimately go too far. If you continue to try and make judo safer and safer, you begin to take the ju-jitsu out of judo, go too far and you will end up with a sport that is little more that a stylized form of choreography. Brazilian ju-jitsu has done a great service to judo. The huge commercial success that Brazilian ju-jitsu has enjoyed should remind judo not to forget the importance of techniques that are effective and relevant to combat. Jigaro Kano got the balance between combat and sport right and there is little, if any, need to try and change what he did.

The success that Brazilian ju-jitsu has enjoyed has had an effect on judo. Many students who may have taken up judo have started to practise Brazilian ju-jitsu because they have been attracted to the new world of mixed martial arts. Fighters from other martial arts that focus mainly on striking techniques, such as boxing, karate and kick-boxing, have started to train in Brazilian ju-jitsu as well in order to improve their grappling skills on the ground. Judo players frustrated by the restrictions judo places upon them on the ground have also started to train in Brazilian ju-jitsu to improve and develop their groundwork skills and become better fighters. Brazilian ju-jitsu has shown judo what is possible in terms of continuing to grow in popularity as a martial art. There is no doubt that Brazilian ju-jitsu fighters are technically superior to those of judo on the ground but there is also no doubt that judo fighters are technically superior to those of Brazilian ju-jitsu in the stand-up position.

Brazilian ju-jitsu and judo were both developed from the ju-jitsu of the samurai warriors of Japan and as such both Brazilian ju-jitsu and judo have much in common. Judo and Brazilian ju-jitsu students technically share many of the same skills and therefore have a common understanding of what they are trying to learn and develop. Combine the technical skills of these two beautiful martial arts and you start to see the complete fighter, someone of the technical brilliance of Mitsuyo Maeda. Brazilian ju-jitsu is an important reminder to judo that ju-jitsu techniques must remain a fundamental part of judo. Ironically, if judo wishes to remain relevant both as a sport and a form of combat, it must look back to its technical roots in ju-jitsu.

Education

The element of combat is what judo has in common with other martial arts but it is the importance of education that distinguishes judo from the rest. Jigaro Kano wanted judo to be more than just a form of combat and to achieve this aim he placed a huge importance on etiquette and manners, both in practice and competition. Etiquette, manners and self-control are still central to judo practice and competition all over the world today. Jigaro Kano wanted judo to help educate people on how they should behave inside and outside the dojo and this aim still remains a central principle to modern judo practice.

The importance of etiquette means that judo has a unique set of manners and customs that are practised by judo players everywhere. This has been incredibly important in unifying judo as an international sport. It has provided clear guidelines for people to come together to train and compete under one universally recognized set of rules and regulations. Judo practice is the same whatever your culture, religion or beliefs. This has been very important to the success of judo abroad and a strong IJF has ensured that judo practice has remained the same all over the world. Today the values of fair play and respect for all are adhered to internationally. Jigaro Kano was a man of vision and very much a man of his time, a time that also saw the birth of the Olympic movement. Jigaro Kano believed in the Olympic movement and he made sure that judo really does reflect the principles that the Olympic movement was founded upon.

The etiquette of judo makes it different from any other sport. All judo classes and competitions will begin and end with a bow. The reason why the bow is so important in judo is because it symbolizes respect for your opponent and yourself. The bow reminds you of the purpose of your practice: the dojo is a place of learning and your practice gives you the opportunity to learn. The bow symbolizes your humility and appreciation for this opportunity to learn and develop. It embodies a spirit of honour, trust and humility. The bow goes right back to the ideals of the samurai and a moral code of practice that should embody how you live your life. This respect for the rules and philosophy of judo is central to the popularity of judo and the success of judo as an international sport. The IJF has got it absolutely right in making sure that each coach, trainer, referee and student understands the importance of proper etiquette. It is the etiquette of judo that brings judo back to one of Jigaro Kano's most important founding principles: education.

It is no accident that Brazilian ju-jitsu may compete with judo in terms of popularity with regard to adult students but has had little effect on the number of children practising judo. Parents bring their children to judo classes because they do not just want their children to learn a sport or how to defend themselves, parents also want their children to learn the moral values, discipline and self-control that are such a central part of judo practice. Taught properly, judo should provide a moral compass as well as a set of technical skills. This moral compass should be a simple set of practical skills that teach each student the value of discipline, hard work and good manners, values that will help anyone in their everyday life. This approach to training and learning means that everything in a judo class and dojo is important.

In the dojo, everything is in the proper place and the proper etiquette is observed at all times. At the centre of this is a code of conduct that insists that all judo players must interact with all other judo players and instructors with respect and courtesy. This structured and simple approach to training is vital to creating the right environment to learn in.

The correct etiquette in judo has created an international language. Wherever you train in the world, each judo class will be structured in the same way and the techniques practised in each class will be referred to by their Japanese name. This attention to detail means that judo players from any country have the same language for each technique and the same code of etiquette and behaviour. A judo class in Russia, Japan or England is run along exactly the same principles and objectives. This really defines Jigaro Kano's original vision for judo, a sport and a form of combat that everyone can practise and learn irrespective of age, creed or culture and that emphasizes the importance of etiquette and education. I leave the final word to the great man himself:

Judo is the way to the most effective use of both physical and spiritual strength. By training you in attacks and defences it refines your body and your soul and helps you make the spiritual essence of judo a part of your very being. In this way you are able to perfect yourself and contribute something of value to the world. This is the final goal of judo discipline.

Jigaro Kano

CHAPTER 2

GETTING STARTED

The first chapter of this book looked at how Jigaro Kano developed the Olympic sport of judo from the martial art of ju-jitsu. The development of judo from ju-jitsu essentially came from the rules and etiquette that Jigaro Kano introduced to the practice of ju-jitsu. These rules and etiquette define what judo is as a sport and how it should be practised. It is therefore important that any new student of judo has some understanding of judo rules and etiquette.

The rules that define judo as a sport are in principle very simple and remain relatively unchanged. There are basically five main ways to win a judo match:

- A competitor can throw their opponent with control from their feet to the ground. For the throw to be successful, a competitor must throw their opponent to the ground with force and velocity so that the opponent lands mainly on their back. This would score an Ippon (10 points) and win the contest.
- If a throw is missing one of these essential elements (control, force, velocity, or on their back), a lesser score is given (a Wazari: 7 points, or a Yuko: 5 points). These scores would not finish a contest; instead, the two competitors would have to fight on until the end of the match (usually 5 minutes). At the end of the match, the winner would be the fighter who had accumulated the most points.
- A competitor throws their opponent to the ground and only scores a Wazari or Yuko, then the fight continues on the ground. If a competitor can then pin their opponent on their back for 25 seconds, they will score an Ippon and win the match. However, if neither fighter can gain an advantage on the ground, the referee will stop the fight and stand the two fighters up. The fight will then be started again from the standing position.
- When fighting on the ground, a competitor can apply pressure to the neck of their opponent in the form of a choke or strangle. This makes the opponent submit or lose consciousness and the competitor will win the contest. However, chokes and strangles can only be practised by adults, not juniors. In judo, you are considered an adult at sixteen years of age.
- When fighting on the ground, a competitor can apply pressure to the arm of their opponent in the form of a lock to the elbow or shoulder joints. This makes the opponent submit or breaks the opponent's arm and the competitor will win the contest. However, arm locks can only be practised by adults, not juniors.

For all judo players, the primary aims of judo are encapsulated in the first three points above. Throw your opponent to the ground with control, force and velocity, land your opponent squarely on their back and win the contest. If you cannot throw your opponent with an Ippon score, because one of these essential elements (control, force, velocity, or on their back) is missing, you follow your opponent to the floor and pin them on their back for 25 seconds.

Submission skills (chokes, strangles and joint locks) are important but are only relevant to adult players. What is more, it is impossible to apply these submission techniques effectively if you have not first established the correct position from which to apply these techniques. In the main, that requires a competitor first to throw and then pin their opponent to the ground. It is only when a competitor has got control of their opponent on the ground that they can usually apply a choke, strangle or arm lock. If a judo player does not have the technical skills first to throw their opponent and then control their opponent on the ground, then they will not be in a position to apply any chokes, strangles or arm locks.

This book covers the fundamentals of judo and will therefore cover the core skills that a judo player needs to have in order to compete. This does not include submission skills (chokes, strangles and arm locks). Instead, this book will focus on the basic throws that any good judo player must learn to be able to throw their opponent and the basic pins that must be learnt to be able to control the opponent on the ground. The techniques discussed in this book are therefore relevant to both junior and senior players. Ten throws and five pins are covered and these specific techniques represent some of the core technical skills that a judo player must master and learn if he or she is going to become a skilled judo player.

Judo is technically a difficult sport to learn and requires a great deal of patience and perseverance. Anyone who wants to become and remain a good judo player must be prepared to put in hours of practice, as there are no shortcuts. However, for many the pay-off in enjoyment and the attainment of a unique set of technical skills make the hours of practice all worthwhile. It is important therefore that any practice is safe and productive. Judo is a fighting martial art and if students simply spend all their time fighting, then there is a high risk of injury and little opportunity to develop a range of technical skills. In judo, there is a time for learning and practising technical skills and a time for competition; both are important.

Jigaro Kano was very precise in the way he structured judo: everything, from the techniques that he wanted taught, to how he wanted people to behave and interact, was detailed and recorded. This precise attention to detail has been vital in defining judo's traditions and customs around the world. For the beginner, the technical complexity of judo and the strange traditions and customs that are part of the structure of every judo class can seem bewildering. This chapter tries to explain why judo is structured the way that it is and how everything has been designed to help a judo player learn and develop.

Etiquette

The correct etiquette is important because how students and instructors behave and interact is key to how they learn. Judo was developed from ju-jitsu and Jigaro Kano's great passion for education, so judo is not just about producing great fighters but also about how we learn and develop as individuals. The correct etiquette in a judo dojo was central to Jigaro Kano's vision because etiquette defines how he wanted judo to be taught. Wherever you train in the world today, a judo class will follow a similar structure and the techniques practised in each class will be referred to by their Japanese name. This means that judo players from any country have the same language for each technique and the same code of etiquette and behaviour. This has led to an international code of conduct that insists that all judo players must interact with all other judo players and instructors with respect and courtesy. The following section gives you an idea of how this works and therefore the practical importance of proper etiquette. This is by no means meant to be a definitive list but instead a useful reference as to what is expected of anyone involved with judo.

1. The Bow

The bow is very important in judo and is a central part of any judo practice or competition. Everyone is expected to perform a standing bow to the centre of the dojo when entering or leaving. This also applies when anyone steps on to the matted area (that makes up the training area) to train or compete; in this case, a standing bow should be made to the centre of the mat. Exactly the same applies when anyone leaves the mat after a competition or training session.

Any judo class will begin with all the students lined up in order of grade. The grade a student has achieved is represented by the colour of the belt that the student wears. Higher grades will be at one end of the line and lower grades at the other end; thus the line is ordered upon technical ability. Facing them are the instructors, who are also lined up in order of their technical ability. Both students and instructors will be in the kneeling position and will bow to one another in the kneeling position at the beginning and end of each class.

A student who is late for a class cannot simply wander on to the matted area when they feel ready to train. Instead he or she must first kneel at the side of the mat and wait. When the instructor gives permission for the student to come on to the matted area, the student must then perform a kneeling bow to the instructor. This sign of respect and humility does not just apply to the relationship between instructor and student, it is also common practice for everyone to perform a standing bow to the person they are training with before and after they practise together.

The bow in judo is symbolically very important and is fundamental to social interaction in Japanese society even today. The standing bow upon entering or leaving the dojo is an important reminder that the dojo is an important place of learning and should be treated as such. The standing bow before going on or leaving the matted training area reminds you of the purpose of your practice and of the opportunity you have to learn. The bow symbolizes your humility and appreciation for this opportunity to learn and develop. It is only by working with fellow students and listening to your instructors that you can improve. So the kneeling bow at the start and end of each class is a commitment by both student and instructor towards using their time together as constructively as possible. It is this idea of teamwork and working together so that everyone can improve that is represented by the bow each student makes to one another before and after they train together. The bow embodies a spirit of honour and trust and goes right back to the ideals of the samurai and to a moral code of practice that should embody how you live your life.

2. Grades

A judo uniform consists of a jacket, trousers and belt. The belt can vary in colour depending upon the technical ability of the person. A beginner will usually wear a red or white belt. As a student progresses and improves so they will grade (pass an exam) and gain a different-coloured belt. There are usually five different belts that a student must gain before a black belt can be obtained. These first five grades are known as Kyu grades and represent beginner or learner. A student can then gain their black belt and this is called their first Dan, meaning 'first step'. The student has now reached a level that means they are no longer a beginner, but this is only recognized as their first step on the path of learning that they have undertaken. A student can go on to become a second Dan, a third Dan and so on, with each level becoming progressively more difficult. At sixth Dan, the colour of the belt will change from black to red and white.

This system of categorizing people according to their technical abilities is very important in judo. The instructor will have a very clear idea of a student's ability without having taught them or met them before. So right from the start, the instructor will know what level of guidance and instruction the student will require. There is also an onus on higher grades to help and look after more junior grades. If a higher grade injures a lower grade in practice, the fault will be considered to be that of the higher grade. If the higher grade is worthy of their grade, they will be able to exercise the skill and control necessary to make sure that their training partner is not injured. Likewise, the junior grade must treat the higher grade with the respect they deserve and view the opportunity to train with a higher grade as an opportunity to learn. This simple code of behaviour embodied in the belt system is very effective in making sure bullies and students who lack self control have no place in a judo class. Everyone has to work hard to achieve their grade and anyone using their judo skills improperly will lose their grade and be expelled from class. The belt system makes it very clear to everyone what is expected of them when it comes to how they should behave inside and outside the dojo.

3. Hygiene

Judo is a grappling martial art like wrestling so there are no strikes, kicks or punches. Instead, judo players grab and hold their opponent in order to throw them to the floor. Once on the floor, the fight continues with each player trying to pin the other down or submit them with a lock, choke or strangle. Judo is therefore a close, physical-contact sport where good personal hygiene is an important requirement. It is essential that everyone has short, clean finger and toenails as this will help prevent

cuts, scratches and turned-back nails. As players use their hands to grab their training partner and try and control their movement, it is also essential that their hands are clean. Keeping the matted training area clean and tidy is a fundamental part of all judo practice and competition. Judo is practiced in bare feet and it is not acceptable to come on to the mat with dirty feet. Most judo players will get changed and then walk from the changing rooms to the matted training area wearing flip-flops or sandals. These are easy to take on or off and must always be worn when a judo player comes to or leaves the mat. This helps to keep the training area free from dirt.

This insistence on a high standard of personal hygiene also extends to clothing. The uniform that a judo player wears (judo gi) must be clean and fit properly. The belt is meant to be tied correctly at all times around your waist. Women or girls are expected to wear a T-shirt or leotard under their judo jacket and no jewellery of any type may be worn.

4. Conduct

The purpose of any code of etiquette is to influence how people behave. Judo etiquette is rooted in the values of budo or bushido, the code of the samurai, a code of behaviour that is based upon good manners, discipline and respect. It is to the credit of judo that many of these trad-itional rules and practices have been retained. Judo is technically not an easy sport to learn, and the practical purpose to good judo etiquette is to help students learn something that is technically difficult and challenging.

In a judo class, you should always face your instructor when they are talking to you and call your instructor 'Sensei' (teacher). You are always expected to be careful and look out for your fellow students. Good manners are a must and foul or violent language will not be tolerated. These simple rules create an environment that helps people learn. However, I believe that the benefits of judo etiquette are not just seen in class but also in the running and governance of judo.

The precise and detailed etiquette of judo has provided clear guidelines for people to come together to train and compete under one universally recognized set of rules and regulations. This has been vital in unifying judo as an inter-national sport. If you look at the problems that other martial arts have had in governing and developing their art as a sport, you begin to understand the important role that etiquette has played in judo. Karate evolved in Japan at the same time as ju-jitsu but karate was not the art of the ruling elite (the samurai) but that of the peasants and farmers who worked the land. However, as with ju-jitsu, there were technical variations to karate depending upon the region of Japan that karate was taught in. Rather than coming together as judo did under one governing body, these different schools of karate remained separate, having nothing to do with one another. This led to a proliferation of different styles of karate around the world, with each style having its own governing body with its own system of grades, competitions and etiquette. Each of the different schools produces their own champions.

It really is important that when judo produces an Olympic or World Champion, that is exactly what they are. Karate, in comparison, cannot do this. What has kept judo unified is that Jigaro Kano was so clear in defining the rules and regulations that still govern judo today. In contrast to many other martial arts, judo has an excellent governing structure, with each country having a national governing body; in the case of Great Britian, the British Judo Association. The national governing body for each country belongs to the governing body for that part of the world, so the BJA is part of the European Judo Union. There are six of these federations representing different parts of the world, such as Africa or Asia, and these bodies make up the International Judo Federation, which governs the sport internationally. It is vital for the continued success of judo that these structures remain strong, well run and unified. The code of conduct Jigaro Kano developed for judo and was so keen to see practised in class and at the Olympic Games helps define how we should continue to run our sport.

Tori and Uke

In judo, Tori executes the throw and Uke is thrown. The relationship between Tori and Uke is a fundamental part of judo practice. It is vital that anyone wanting to learn judo understands the importance of this relationship and the code of conduct that defines it.

Most judo throws require a good deal of practice before Tori is able to execute the throw properly. To develop the complex motor skills that are necessary to throw Uke, Tori will need to throw Uke many, many times. Each time Tori executes a throw in practice, she must exercise control and restraint; if not, then it is likely that Uke will get injured. Injure too many training partners and no one will want to practise with you and training will not be something to enjoy or look forward to. Judo is primarily a sport and the objective should not be to injure your training partner or your opponent. It is therefore important that Tori and Uke work together in training and help one another.

Uke does not just provide Tori with a body to practise on and throw repeatedly to the ground. Uke can give Tori feedback and help Tori understand what she may be doing wrong. Judo skills need to be practised at a level that helps Tori learn, because if Tori keeps making the same mistake,

then she is not learning the technique correctly. Uke can help Tori pinpoint what she is doing wrong. In judo practice, Tori and Uke should always work together in a controlled environment in order to help each other learn and develop.

If Tori is trying to learn a specific throw in training, Uke should fully understand what Tori is trying to do and what his role is. When Tori first starts to practise a new technique, the technique should be broken down into the correct stages. These stages should then be performed slowly until the skill becomes assimilated into the muscle memory. Tori can then put these stages together to form one sequence of movements that make up a particular technique. This process should never be forced or rushed. Uke's role is to help Tori during this process and deliver the proper movement responses to Tori's attack. If Uke does not understand his role in practice, Tori will find it much more difficult to practise and learn the correct technique.

Giving and receiving feedback is an important part of learning judo. Judo has always placed considerable importance on learning and creating the right environment in which to learn and develop. As a result, judo practice focuses on the acquisition of technical skill and not just fighting. The relationship between Tori and Uke is central to this theme of learning and development. Judo skills need to be practised in an environment that is safe and where the technique can be repeated over and over again. Tori and Uke must work together if this is going to be achieved.

When Tori first learns a throw, Uke is cooperative and lets Tori throw him. This helps Tori because Tori can focus on the precise movements necessary to execute the throw correctly. As Tori develops the skills necessary to execute the throw properly, Uke can then provide some resistance and therefore make Tori work on the skills necessary to set the throw up. Tori will now have to move Uke around the mat and break his balance (see the section below on Breaking Balance) to provide the opportunity he needs to perform the throw. In this situation, Uke is helping Tori develop the skills necessary to execute the throw on the move and under pressure. Uke may even attack Tori so that Tori can learn how to use a particular throw as a counter to an opponent's attack. All these skills are an essential part of the learning process that Tori must go through to learn a throw properly. A good Uke is an essential part of this process.

The following points will define the relationship between Tori and Uke:

• The first stage to learning a judo throw is for Uke to be co-operative and let Tori throw him. At this stage, Tori can practise the set sequence of movements that make up the throw and Uke can practise the breakfalls that he will need to execute if he is to fall safely. It is only after this stage of learning has been mastered properly that both Tori and Uke should move on to performing the throw on the move. Each description and analysis of the throws detailed in this book will start from the beginning and assume that Tori and Uke are working together co-operatively. If Tori and Uke are sensible and work together, they will learn and progress. When Tori practises any throw, it is important that Uke understands which breakfall she must perform. A breakfall is the movement Uke uses to protect himself when thrown by Tori. Performed correctly, the breakfall allows Uke to fall safely and Tori to practise the throw properly. The description of each throw in this book will detail which breakfall Uke must perform when Tori throws him. It is therefore really important that you read the section on Breakfalls below and that Uke understands what role he must play in practice.

For the purposes of this book, Tori is a girl and Uke a boy. If I refer to 'she' or 'her', I am referring to Tori; if I refer to

Fig. 2 Uke.

'he' or 'him', I am referring to Uke. I hope this will help clarify the different roles of Tori and Uke when I come to the technical descriptions of the throws and pins detailed in this book. Tori will be dressed in a blue gi and Uke in a white gi. This will make it easier to identify who is Tori and who is Uke in any pictures.

Grips

One of the most important pieces of equipment in judo is the gi. The gi is the uniform that all judo players wear in practice and competition. The gi consists of a jacket, trousers and belt. The gi was developed from the Japanese kimono and evolved into the form of clothing that all judo players wear in training and competition. The gi material is strong and designed so that it does not tear with all the gripping, pushing and pulling involved in judo.

In judo, Tori will grip Uke's gi with both hands in order to throw him. The standard or traditional judo grip is known as the sleeve and lapel grip, a grip that can be done

Fig. 1 Tori.

Fig. 3 The gi.

using the same side grips. However, if Tori uses a right-handed grip and Uke uses a left-handed grip, then they are using opposing grips.

To throw Uke, Tori needs to achieve two things. First, Tori must put Uke's body in the correct position to be thrown. Second, Tori must then put her body in the correct positi on from which to execute the throw. It is essential, therefore, that Tori can control the direction in which Uke moves his body and place Uke in the position she wants to throw him from, while at the same time getting her body in to the correct position from which to throw Uke. Tori's grip and how she uses her hands are vital parts of this process.

There is a huge variety of grips that a judo player can use, which can generally be divided into orthodox and unorthodox grips. An orthodox grip is basically the sleeve

left- or right-handed. For a right-handed grip, Tori would grip the left lapel of Uke's jacket with her right hand and the right sleeve of Uke's jacket with her left hand. For a left-handed grip, the roles of the hands are simply reversed. Tori would grip the right lapel of Uke's jacket with her left hand and the left sleeve of Uke's jacket with her right hand.

The hand that grips the lapel of Uke's jacket is called the fishing hand (tsurite). Tori will tend to use the fishing hand to pull or push Uke. The hand that grips the sleeve is called the pulling hand (hikite). Tori will tend to use the pulling hand to draw Uke forward or around.

Although the action of the fishing and pulling hands are different, the two hands work in tandem. It is vital that when the fishing hand is pushing Uke, the pulling hand is also pulling Uke. This is particularly important when Tori is trying to break Uke's balance (see the section below on Breaking Balance) and therefore put Uke in the correct position from which to throw him.

When Tori and Uke both grip each other's gi with a traditional, right-handed, sleeve and lapel grip, they are

Fig. 4 A right-handed traditional sleeve and lapel grip.

Fig. 5 An orthodox grip.

Fig. 6 An unorthodox grip.

and lapel grip and any recognizable variation of this particular grip. So a grip such as the sleeve and collar grip would be considered an orthodox grip.

As a judo player develops and becomes more skilful, the grips used can become much more complicated. Many of the very top competitors use grips that they have developed themselves or in conjunction with their coach. Such grips would be referred to as unorthodox grips. An example of an unorthodox grip would be Tori reaching over Uke's back with her fishing hand to grab Uke's belt.

As this book deals with the fundamentals of judo, the focus will be on the use of orthodox grips. If a judo player cannot first throw their opponent with an orthodox grip, it is highly unlikely that they will be able to throw their opponent with an unorthodox grip. Changing grips and using unorthodox grips mainly concern the specific strategies and tactics of judo players competing at the highest level and are therefore outside the compass of this book. However, the grip is an important part of judo and is treated as such here.

The description of each throw in this book will have a section on the grip. The description of the grip for each throw will make the following assumptions:

- Where possible, Tori will use the traditional sleeve and lapel grip. This is the most common grip in judo and the grip that is taught particularly to beginners. I recommend that everyone should start with this grip. For the description of each grip, I will assume that Tori is right-handed. For the traditional sleeve and lapel grip, this means that Tori would grip the left lapel of Uke's jacket with her right hand and the right sleeve of Uke's jacket with her left hand. If Tori wanted to use a left-handed grip, then the roles of the hands are simply reversed.

Breakfalls

One of the basic objectives of judo is to throw your opponent or training partner to the ground. Judo is primarily a throwing art and it is therefore inevitable that anyone who practises the sport will be thrown over and over again. One of the biggest barriers to enjoying judo is a fear of being thrown and getting hurt. If anyone wants to enjoy their judo and remain injury free then they must be able to fall correctly and without fear when they are thrown. A fundamental skill that must be mastered by anyone who wants to enjoy and develop their judo is the breakfall.

If you attend and watch a judo class anywhere in the world, a significant part of the class will be devoted to students falling over again and again. This is because any judo player must regularly practise the movements involved in being thrown. These breakfalls are the fundamental skills any judo player must develop if they are to be thrown with force to the ground and remain confident and injury free. There are four basic breakfalls that every judo player must know and practise.

1. Ushiro Ukemi (Backwards Breakfall)

The objective of a backward breakfall is simply to fall backwards to the floor without injury. In practice, this means that it is particularly important to protect your head and wrists from injury. As a person falls backwards they tend to instinctively do two things:

- They allow the force of the fall to throw their head backwards.
- They throw their hands out to either side to help break the force of the fall.

The result is that the two things that hit the ground first and therefore absorb most of the force of the fall are the back of the head and the wrists.

The back of the head and the wrists are not designed to hit the ground heavily and take the weight of your falling body. Usually what happens when a person falls like this is that they get concussion and/or a broken wrist and these are the consequences if you do not fall backwards

Fig. 8 Ushiro Ukemi with a backwards roll.

properly in judo. To fall backwards properly, it is essential that you tuck your head in so that your chin is touching your chest and that you do not put your hands out to the side. Ideally you want to land on your bottom and roll backwards on to your back. You want your bottom to hit the mat first as this is far less likely to fracture than your wrists. Judo players will practise Ushiro Ukemi again and again so that it becomes instinctive for them to tuck their head in, push their bottom out and not throw their hands out to the side when they are thrown backwards.

A good judo player will slap the mat with straight arms after landing on the ground. This is to help dissipate the force of the fall and to alert other judo players on the mat that you have been thrown and are now on the floor. You would not slap the floor with your hands if you had fallen on a hard surface such as concrete. Slapping the mat is a custom unique to training on a matted surface.

If you look at Figure 7, the judo player has her bottom sticking out and she is almost sitting down as she falls backwards. What she does not do is stand tall and fall stiff like a tree or a pole. Her head is tucked in so when she hits the floor and rolls back, her head does not touch the mat. The force of the fall is absorbed by her bottom and back with the arms coming down to her side as her back touches the mat.

You can roll backwards out of the breakfall into the standing position. This is useful because it can help dissipate the force of the throw and help you regain a standing fighting stance as quickly as possible. If you look at Figure 8, the judo player has put both her legs to the same side of her head. So as her body rolls back over her head, both her legs pass over the same shoulder, thus protecting her neck. The head and the neck are the two parts of the body

Fig. 7 Ushiro Ukemi.

that are vulnerable to injury if this is not done properly. If the legs are split (similar to the ten to two position on a clock), and pass either side of the head as you roll over, then you put a much greater strain on the neck. The judo player in Figure 8 has avoided this by bringing both her legs over the same shoulder. This makes the whole movement much more fluid, relaxed and less prone to injury.

This is a great skill to practise in the warm-up because it prepares the body for the more strenuous exercise that will come later on in the class as well as refining the skills you need to protect your body when you are also thrown later on in the class. There are many different warm-up drills designed to help you practise Ushiro Ukemi but all will concentrate on the application of good technique.

2. Mae Mawari Ukemi (Front-Rolling Breakfall)

Mae Mawari Ukemi means front-rolling breakfall and mimics the action of being thrown by a hip or shoulder throw. It is therefore a fundamental judo skill that must be practised over and over again. If you are not able to master Mae Mawari Ukemi, then you will always be vulnerable to injury when you are thrown. If you are confident and relaxed when you practise Mae Mawari Ukemi, it is much more likely you will be the same when you are thrown.

To the untrained eye, Mae Mawari Ukemi looks to be a fairly complex skill to master but it is not so different from a forward roll. If you cannot do a forward roll properly, then you are going to struggle to do Mae Mawari Ukemi properly. This is because the basic principles of the two movements are essentially the same. If you look at Figure 9, Tori is standing with her feet shoulder-width apart and in line. Her legs are slightly bent and her chin is tucked into her chest. Her arms are stretched out in front of her at about shoulder height and are slightly bent. She bends her torso forward and pushes with her legs, the hands touch the mat first and allow her to bring her legs over her head. It is the back of the shoulder blades that touch the mat first and because she is in the tuck position she continues to roll until she is back on her feet.

The important principles here are that the head is tucked in and that the head does not touch the mat. It is the back of the shoulders that first make contact with the mat. Similarly, when Mae Mawari ukemi is performed properly, it is the head that must be protected so it is essential that the head does not make contact with the mat. It is the back of the leading shoulder that must make contact with the mat first as Tori rolls over.

A major difference between a forward roll and Mae Mawari Ukemi is the position of the feet when you start the movement. If you look at Figure 10, Tori still has her feet shoulder-width apart but her feet are no longer in line. Instead she has taken a step forward, in this case with her right foot. This simple adjustment often confuses students, and instead of rolling forward from this position they twist their body so that they make a roly-poly kind of movement. To stop this happening, Tori has her right arm out in front, slightly bent, with the palm of her hand facing away from her face. The arm is in this position to help guide Tori when she rolls forward. Tori tucks her head in and rolls over her right shoulder. It is vital that the head does not touch the mat, that the back of the judo players's right shoulder touches the mat first, that the right arm only guides the judo player through the roll and that the right arm or shoulder does not bear any of the impact.

Again, Mae Mawari Ukemi is a great skill to practise

Fig. 9 Forward roll.

Fig. 10 Mae Mawari Ukemi.

during the warm-up of a class. It gets the body warm and ready for more intense exercise and prepares the body for the shock of being thrown later on. Judo players will practise this skill over and over again because it is a central skill to being safe and confident in your judo training whatever your level of ability or age.

3. Mae Ukemi (Front Breakfall)

This breakfall is the breakfall that new students find the most difficult to master. It is difficult because the technique demands that you overcome the natural instinct to throw your arms out in front of you and let your hands take most of the impact when you hit the ground. The instinct kicks in because of the fear that when you fall forward your face may hit the ground. It is logical to feel that the further your arms are stretched out in front of you, the better your face will be protected. However, the wrists are not designed to take your weight when you fall forward. If you fall forward and you land in what I would call the press-up position, it is your hands and wrists that will bear the brunt of your weight. Damage or fracture to the wrists or hands is the most likely outcome.

This instinctive or reflex action is a learnt action. If you look at a small child (about the age of three) running on the mat, the child will almost certainly trip up over their feet and fall forward. A small child never lands in the press-up position; instead, they will fall on to their arms, chest and stomach. Small children fall over a lot but are rarely injured as they naturally breakfall very well. Mae Ukemi technically is similar to what we did as three-year-olds, and as judo students we usually have to relearn how to fall forward and overcome our fear of banging our face on the floor and stop ourselves throwing our hands out.

Figure 11 shows the finishing position for Mae Ukemi.

The arms are in the shape of a triangle with the hands almost touching and the elbows slightly wider than either side of the body. The forearms are the part of the arms that take the force of the fall. In Figure 11, you can see that the hands are facing downwards and the arm from the hand to the elbow is in contact with the mat. This triangle shape of the arms makes the braking force of the arms stronger and should prevent the head from coming into contact with the floor. However, Tori has turned her head to the side in order to protect the face further. The head should not touch the floor but if the fall or throw is too powerful and Tori cannot prevent her head from striking the ground, then turning the head to the side will give more protection to the face.

The triangle shape made by the arms not only increases the breaking force provided by the arms but also provides the strength necessary for Tori to keep the rest of her body off the ground. If you look at Figure 11, her chest, hips and knees are all off the ground; this obviously helps protect the body from the full force of the fall or throw.

It is very important to remember at the start of this breakfall not to fall forward stiff and rigid like a pole. As we get older, our fear of falling makes us instinctively stiffen as we fall and unfortunately this actually increases our likelihood of getting injured. The body needs to relaxed and flexible if you are to maximize the body's ability to absorb the force of a fall or throw effectively. So at the start of this breakfall it is important that Tori bends her legs and pushes forward as if she was diving into a swimming pool. The arms should be in front, in a triangle shape, bent at the elbow with the hands pointing downwards. The triangle shape of the arms should provide the strength necessary to break the fall, while the rest of the body should be relaxed and loose.

Fig. 11 Mae Ukemi.

Fig. 12 Yoko Ukemi.

4. Yoko Ukemi (Side Breakfall)

The primary goal of all breakfalls is to disperse the force of a fall or throw throughout the entire body and to protect the head. The primary goal of Yoko Ukemi is the same, but whereas the wrists and head have been particularly vulnerable to injury with the other three breakfalls it is the shoulder joint that is vulnerable to injury with Yoko Ukemi. This is because the temptation is to finish in a position where the upper body is propped up from the floor by the upper arm. It is a position we all use when we are lying on our side on the floor watching television or reading a book. Our legs and hips lie flat against the floor, but by bending our arm and putting our elbow against the floor we prop up our head and shoulders from the floor with our upper arm. If you land in this position with Yoko Ukemi, then the downward force of the throw or fall will damage your shoulder. The shoulder is not a joint designed to absorb such shearing forces. If you look at Tori in Figure 12, she has landed on her side but it is the back of her shoulder (the shoulder blade) that is in contact with the mat. It is vital that this is the position you finish in. In this position, the force of the throw or fall is dissipated throughout the entire body and the shoulder is protected. Notice that just as with Ushiro and Mae Mawari Ukemi, Tori has tucked her head in so that the head remains protected and never touches the mat.

When you fall to the side it is again important not to fall stiff and rigid like a pole. It is the hips and buttocks that should meet the mat first and then the upper body and back of the shoulder. In Figure 13, Tori is starting the fall from the kneeling position. This is a great way to start learning Yoko Ukemi because this starting position allows the beginner to feel safe, and it therefore gives her

confidence and helps her land in the correct position. Tori starts the breakfall by bringing the front leg (the leg where the knee is not touching the ground) across her body. This leg is no longer supporting her body so she falls sideways

Fig. 13 Yoko Ukemi from kneeling.

to her right. Her hips and buttocks hit the mat first and then her upper body. As she starts to fall, Tori pulls her right arm across her body so that her right hand is pointing to her left-hand side. This pulls her right shoulder across her body, thereby making it easier for her to fall on to the back of her right shoulder. When she has hit the floor, then and only then does she use her right hand to slap the mat.

The routine is exactly the same when Tori performs this breakfall from standing. In Figure 12, Tori has fallen on to her right side. To fall onto her right side she will bring her right leg across the front of her body. The right leg is therefore no longer supporting her weight so she falls to the right. Her hips and buttocks hit the mat first and then her upper body. Just as when she was in the kneeling position, she pulls her right arm across her body as she starts to fall. This pulls her right shoulder across her body, thereby making it easier for her to fall on to the back of her right shoulder. When she has finished the breakfall, she then uses her right hand to slap the mat.

The Importance of Breakfalls

You will get thrown over and over again in judo. There is nothing to fear from being thrown and there is no reason you should be injured if you can breakfall correctly. The breakfall is a fundamental skill that must be mastered by anyone who wants to enjoy and develop their judo. If you cannot breakfall well, you will always be prone to getting hurt or injured when you are practising or competing.

Many beginners in judo do not spend the necessary time learning and practising their breakfalls. As a result, their technique is poor and their confidence suffers. Judo should be a sport that you really enjoy. As a coach, I want my students to look forward to their judo practice and and this will not happen if a student is frightened of being thrown. It is essential that any judo player has good fundamental skills starting with excellent technique in their breakfalls. These skills will give all judo players the confidence and ability to go on and really enjoy their judo for years to come. Breakfalls are a great way of warming up for a training session and most judo classes will start with Ukemi (breakfall) practice. This can at time seem repetitious but it is with good reason. Look after your breakfalls with regular practice and your breakfalls will look after you when it really matters.

When Tori practises a throw, it is important that Uke understands which breakfall he must perform. Performed correctly, the breakfall will allow Uke to fall safely and Tori to practise the throw properly. The description of each throw in this book will detail which breakfall Uke must perform when Tori throws him. It is important that Uke understands the role he will play in practice and therefore how he can protect himself.

Breaking Your Opponent's Balance

The main technical focus of judo, in comparison to other martial arts, is on throwing your opponent to the ground. Technically, there are two important factors that any student must understand in order to execute a judo throw correctly. The first is that any judo player must first put their body in the correct position to be able to throw someone. The description and breakdown of each throw in the following chapter of this book will deal with what you have to do in detail to achieve this. The second factor is that any judo player must also be able to put their opponent in the correct position to be thrown. This second point is complex because to execute a throw correctly you need to control both the movement of your body and your opponent's body. You can attack and execute a throw perfectly against your opponent but if your opponent has both feet firmly planted on the ground and has good balance (often referred to as a good base), your attack is unlikely to succeed. You need to set your opponent up for the throw before you attack. Breaking your opponent's balance before you throw them is a fundamental and essential part of the technical skill that all judo throws require if they are to be executed successfully.

In judo terms, you have good balance if you are in the standing position and the trunk of your body is held directly above your feet. Your feet are approximately shoulder-width apart and the weight of your body is evenly distributed between your feet. However, if your body is pulled or pushed (especially the upper part of your body), it is not easy for you to retain this posture and therefore your balance. To retain your balance you must move your feet. If you are pulled forward, you will step forward with one leg to retain your balance. When your leading leg is placed firmly on the ground in front of you, then you have regained your balance. You have good balance or base but one foot is further in front than the other. Your feet are still approximately shoulder-width apart and the weight of your body evenly distributed between the feet. If you are pushed backwards, you will step back with one leg to retain your balance. When your leg is placed firmly on the ground behind you, then you will have regained your balance. You now have good balance or base but one foot is further behind than the other. The feet are still approximately shoulder-width apart and the weight of the body evenly distributed between the feet.

This is one of the reasons that the feet are kept approximately shoulder-width apart in judo because this stance always forms a good base for the body and therefore helps maintain good balance. You need to move in judo because judo is a dynamic sport performed on the move. When you move, you must transfer your body weight from one leg to another. When you are transferring your body weight from one leg to another, then in judo terms your balance is broken. This is because your weight is no longer evenly distributed between your feet, and your feet are no longer firmly planted to the ground. To regain your balance, you must return to the situation where both your feet are firmly planted on the ground and your weight is evenly distributed between your feet.

When you move in judo, you do not want to take big steps and you do not want to lift your feet far from the ground as both these actions will make you vulnerable to attack. You want to move easily and swiftly so that the weight of the body can be transferred from one foot to the other as quickly as possible and good balance re-gained. It is when your balance is broken and you are transferring your weight from one leg to the other that your opponent will try and throw you.

The simplest example of breaking the balance is when someone steps on a banana skin and this is an analogy I will return to many times in this book. You take a step forward, your body weight is mainly on your back leg and this allows you to push forward with your leading leg. As you push your leading leg forward, your body weight is transferred from your back leg to your front leg. Your leading leg is now bearing most of your body weight and makes contact with the ground but you cannot plant the foot of the leading leg firmly down on the ground because there is a banana skin there. The banana skin makes the foot of the leading leg slide away so that you cannot place your weight on this foot but, nevertheless, your weight is committed to this foot. You cannot retain your balance and you fall over.

Quite simply, a judo throw is the banana skin. You get your opponent to transfer his or her weight in a certain direction and then you apply your judo throw as he or she is transferring their weight. The throw simply ensures that your opponent never regains their balance and has to fall to the floor. An essential skill to judo, therefore, is the ability to break your opponent's balance, while you retain your own balance. If you have broken your opponent's balance correctly, then it will require relatively little effort to throw your opponent, which is why judo is often trans-lated as 'the gentle way'. The complex part is that there are eight different directions in which you can break your opponent's balance and each direction lends itself to a different judo throw.

The first step to understanding how to break your opponent's balance is to practise with an opponent who is passive, so this section will look at the different tech-niques of breaking your opponent's balance when they are standing still. However, judo is a dynamic and explosive sport and it is important that you also learn how to apply these skills when your opponent is on the move. By moving your opponent, they will risk their balance because

they must transfer their weight from one leg to another to produce movement. The principle here is to synchronize your movement with your opponent's movement in the same direction. This can be done with an attack by you or by simply yielding to the force of your opponent's attack. Such action, if accompanied by the correct balance breaker, will prevent your opponent from moving their feet in the direction they need to in order to regain their balance. This will provide you with the perfect opportunity with which to throw your opponent to the ground. Learn how to break the balance when your opponent is static so that you develop good technique, but then go on to develop these skills on the move.

How to Break Your Opponent's Balance

In general, there are two ways of breaking your oppon-ent's balance.

The first way is to attack your opponent and use force to break their balance. To do this correctly, you should use your whole body as a lever and either push your oppon-ent backwards or pull your opponent forward. A lever is most effective if it is used to push an object backwards or to pull an object forward. Exactly the same principle applies if you use your body as a lever to break your opponent's balance. However, it is essential to remember that the driving or pulling power of the body is derived from the weight of the whole body and not from just the arms or legs. Use the whole of your body to bring your opponent forward or to drive them backwards because this is the most efficient way to use your body as a lever to break your opponent's balance. 'Efficient' here means breaking your opponent's balance with the minimum of effort.

The second way is to use the force of your opponent's attack to break their balance. In this case, it is important to relax the muscles of your body so that your body is flex-ible. Then the force applied by your opponent can be deflected and turned against them. If your opponent pushes you and you move back faster than your opponent can move forward, then your opponent will topple forward. If your opponent pulls you forward and you move forward faster than your opponent can move backwards, then your opponent will topple backwards. Once again, you have used your body as a lever to break your oppon-ent's balance but this time you also used the momentum generated from your opponent's attack to help you main-tain your balance and break your opponent's balance.

This second method of breaking an opponent's balance is much more difficult to learn because ithe student requires a greater degree of experience. I would advise any student to first learn how to break an opponent's balance by force before moving on to the second scenario and using the force of the opponent's attack to break their balance. The first scenario is usually used when you are attacking your opponent; the second scenario is usually used as a counter to an opponent's attack. A counter-attack requires a much higher level of skill and an appreciation of tactics. For the purpose of this book, it is important first to cover the principles of using force to break your opponent's balance. For each of the ten throws described in this book, Tori will use force to break Uke's balance. How Tori achieves this will be detailed in the description for each of these throws.

However, in judo you do not just move your opponent forward or backwards to break their balance. There are eight different directions in which you can break your opponent's balance and pushing your opponent back-wards or pulling your opponent forward covers only two of these directions. For a lever to move an object in a different direction, other than just forward or backwards, a rotational force must also be applied. Therefore, to move your opponent backwards and to the side, you would need to push your opponent backwards and apply a rota-tional force at the same time. To move your opponent forward and to the side, you would need to pull your opponent forward and again apply a rotational force at the same time.

If you place your hands on your opponent's shoulders and your opponent places their hands on your shoulders, the two of you form a ring. To break your opponent's balance, turn this ring in the same way you would turn the steering wheel of a car. If you turn anticlockwise, your right hand should push forward and your left hand should pull backwards at the same time and at the same speed. If you also step backwards with your left foot at the same time, you will draw your opponent forward and to the side. However, if instead you step forward with the right foot, at the same time that you move your hands, then you will force your opponent backwards and to the side. You must move at least one of your feet backwards or forward when you turn your opponent, as you must use the whole of your body weight to break your opponent's balance and not just your hands.

Applying a Balance Breaker

The action of a throw should be one continuous move-ment, but when we learn how to perform a throw we break the movement down into stages to make it easier to learn the exact movements involved. Every throw must have an opening before the throw can be applied and each opening is created by breaking your opponent's balance. The movement that causes your opponent to fall to the ground is the throw; breaking the balance is the movement that makes the throw possible. Most balance breakers are designed to cause your opponent to balance on their toes or heel because your opponent cannot

balance properly if they cannot put their feet firmly on the ground.

This process is often compared to balancing a heavy box on its corner. The corner of the box is not able to provide a stable base for the box and therefore support the full weight of the box. If you let go of the box, the box will inevitably fall on to one of its sides and essentially regain its balance. You require a considerable degree of control and subtleness to balance this box on one of its corners. If your pull is too strong, the box will fall forward on top of you; if you push too hard, the box will simply fall away from you; and if you relax too much and lose control of the box, the box will fall on its side and regain its balance. The skill and control required to break your opponent's balance and keeping control of your oppon-ent's body in judo is very similar to keeping this box balanced on one corner.

With very few exceptions, the completion of your balance breaker should mean that your opponent is now balancing on their toes, heels or one foot. By then placing yourself in a suitable position and adopting the correct posture, you can throw your opponent to the ground. However, you must not lose control of your opponent's body at any stage, otherwise they will be able to escape. A balance breaker can be executed in any direction, but for convenience it is studied and practised in eight different directions.

The application of the throw is similar to tipping our box over an obstacle. An example of this would be tipping your opponent over your hips (the obstacle) for a hip throw. For this to work, the obstacle must be placed at a point lower than the centre of gravity of the box. This is why in judo it is so important that many balance breakers draw your opponent up and on to their toes because this action raises your opponent's centre of gravity. When you then place yourself in a suitable position to execute the throw, you can bend your legs to make sure that your centre of gravity is lower that of your opponent. This allows you to execute the throw correctly and with the minimum of effort.

It is impossible to exaggerate the importance of break-ing your opponent's balance. It is fundamental to the successful application of technique. Below I have described the eight different directions to breaking your opponent's balance. Each technique should be practised in isolation with your training partner standing still. However, when you are comfortable with each technique, you should then practise each technique on the move. Once you are comfortable with each technique on the move, you should then add a throw to the end of each technique. This should mean that, with practice, each balance breaker will flow effortlessly into a throw.

The Eight Directions to Breaking Balance

In the following section Tori is breaking Uke's balance (see the section on Tori and Uke in Chapter 2). Tori is a girl and dressed in a blue gi, Uke is a boy and dressed in a white gi. Tori starts all the balance breakers detailed below with a traditional sleeve and lapel, right-handed grip. So Tori is gripping Uke's right sleeve with her left hand and gripping the left lapel of Uke's jacket with her right hand. The direction of the balance breaker is relative to Uke. So to the right means to Uke's right and to the front means to Uke's front.

1. To the Front

Uke is drawn forward and up on to the tips of his toes. In this position, just the slightest touch would be enough to cause Uke to fall forward. This balance breaker is the classic opening for a hip or shoulder throw. Tori is in a well-balanced position. The knees are slightly bent and the feet shoulder-width apart. The trunk of the body is in a nice upright posture and Tori is not looking down. In practice, this balance breaker should be used when the opponent moves forward.

2. To the Right Front Corner

Just as with the first balance breaker, Uke is drawn forward and up on to his toes. However, Uke is not just drawn forward but is also drawn to his right. This means that the majority of Uke's weight is over his right leg, so that in effect he is balanced on the toes of his right foot. This balance breaker is another good opening for different hip throws as well as some hand throws, such as Tai Otoshi.

The posture and action of Tori is very similar to the first balance breaker. The fundamental difference is that Tori has turned her body so that the right side of her body is facing her opponent. She achieves this by drawing her left foot back and around to the right, and this movement effectively turns her body through 90 degrees. It also creates the space for Uke's body to move forward into. The pull of Tori's left hand on Uke's right sleeve is very important in drawing Uke forward. This balance breaker is best applied when Uke takes a step forward with his right foot.

Fig. 14 Breaking the balance to the front.

Fig. 15 Breaking the balance to the right front corner.

3. To the Right Side

Tori makes Uke balance on his right foot. Uke is literally pinned to the mat because all of his weight is balanced on the right leg. Take the leg away and it is obviously impossible for Uke to remain standing. This balance breaker is a good opening for hand throws such as Tai Otoshi.

To break Uke's balance, Tori takes a step to her left. In stepping to the left it is important that Tori does not bring her feet together. If Tori brings her feet together, she will have sacrificed her balance in trying to break Uke's balance and she will be vulnerable to being thrown herself. It is important that in moving Uke to his right, Tori takes the first step to the side with her left foot. By keeping her feet shoulder-width apart, she will retain her balance and drive Uke's weight up and on to his right leg. Tori's hands play a crucial role in this process. As Tori steps to the side, she turns her hands as if she were turning the wheel of a ship. The right hand (which is gripping Uke's lapel) will drive upwards, and the left hand (which is gripping Uke's sleeve) will drive downwards.

4. To the Right Back Corner

Tori forces Uke backwards so that he has to balance his weight primarily on the heel of his right foot. His body is bent backwards and his head is over the right foot. This is a classic opening for throws such as O Soto Gari.

To move Uke back and on to his right leg, Tori takes a diagonal step forward with her left foot. This diagonal step brings Tori to the side of Uke. Tori's left hand pulls Uke to his right, bringing Uke's weight over his right leg. It is important that Tori's left hand does not pull downwards as this will help Uke balance his weight on his right leg. Instead, Tori should pull slightly upwards with the left hand as this will help keep Uke on the heel of his right foot and therefore unbalanced.

Tori uses her right hand to pull Uke close to her. This allows her to use the lever effect of her body that I described earlier. By pulling Uke close to her, Tori can use the whole of her body weight to drive Uke back and to the right as she takes her diagonal step forward.

Fig. 16 Breaking the balance to the right side.

Fig. 17 Breaking the balance to the right back corner.

Fig. 18 Breaking the balance to the back.

5. To the Back

Tori pushes Uke backwards so Uke is forced to balance on the heels of his feet. In this position, just the slightest touch would be enough to cause Uke to fall backwards. This balance breaker is a good opening for leg throws such O Uchi Gari.

To drive Uke's body backwards, Tori takes a step forward with her right foot. When Tori steps forward she keeps the trunk of her body upright and does not look down. This posture allows Tori to use her whole body to drive Uke backwards. As Tori steps forward, she also uses her right arm to drive Uke back.

6. To the Left Back Corner

Tori forces Uke backwards so that he has to balance his weight primarily on the heel of his left foot. His body is bent backwards and his head is over his left foot. This is a classic opening for throws such as O Soto Gake.

To move Uke back and on to his left leg, Tori takes a diagonal step forward with her right foot. This diagonal step brings Tori to the side of Uke. Tori's right hand pulls Uke to his left, bringing Uke's weight over his left leg. It is important that Tori's right hand does not pull downwards

Fig. 19 Breaking the balance to the left back corner.

as this will help Uke balance his weight on his left leg. Instead, Tori should pull slightly upwards with the right hand as this will help keep Uke on the heel of his left foot and therefore unbalanced.

Tori uses her left hand to pull Uke close to her. This allows her to use the lever effect of her body that I described earlier. By pulling Uke close to her, Tori can use the whole of her body weight to drive Uke back and to the left as she takes her diagonal step forward.

7. To the Left Side

This time Tori makes Uke balance on his left foot. Uke is pinned to the mat because all of his weight is balanced on the left leg. Take the leg away and it is impossible for Uke to remain standing. This balance breaker is a good opening for hand throws such as Tai Otoshi.

To break Uke's balance, Tori takes a step to her right. In stepping to the right, it is important that Tori does not bring her feet together. If Tori brings her feet together, she will have sacrificed her balance in trying to break Uke's balance and she will be vulnerable to being thrown herself. It is important that in moving Uke to his left, Tori takes the

Fig. 20 Breaking the balance to the left side.

Fig. 21 Breaking the balance to the right front corner.

first step to the side with her right foot. By keeping her feet shoulder-width apart, she will retain her balance and drive Uke's weight up and on to his left leg. Tori's hands play a crucial role in this process. As Tori steps to the side, she turns her hands as if she were turning the wheel of a ship. The left hand (which is gripping Uke's sleeve) will drive upwards and the right hand (which is gripping Uke's lapel) will drive downwards.

8. To the Left Front Corner

Just as with the first balance breaker, Uke is drawn forward and up on to his toes. However, Uke is not just drawn forward but is also drawn to his left. This means that the majority of Uke's weight is over his left leg, so that in effect he is balanced on the toes of his left foot. This balance breaker is another good opening for different hip throws as well as some hand throws, such as Tai Otoshi.

The posture and action of Tori are very similar to the first balance breaker. The fundamental difference is that Tori has turned her body so that the left side of her body is facing Uke. She achieves this by drawing her right foot back and around to the left, and this movement effectively turns her body through 90 degrees. It also creates the space for Uke's body to move forward into. The pull of Tori's right hand on Uke's left lapel is very important in drawing Uke forward. This balance breaker is best applied when Uke takes a step forward with his left foot.

CHAPTER 3

THROWS (TACHI-WAZA)

The main technical focus of judo is to throw your opponent to the ground so that they land on their back with force and velocity. The purpose of this chapter is to introduce the reader to the core throws that help form the basis of the Kodokan judo syllabus, the syllabus that Jigaro Kano started to develop around 100 years ago.

The action for each of the throws described in this book should be one continuous movement, but when we learn how to perform a throw we break the movement down into stages to make it easier to learn the exact chain of movements that are involved. Each stage should then be practised until the skill becomes assimilated into the muscle memory. You can then put these stages together to form one sequence of movement that makes up a particular throw. In this book, each throw is broken down in to the following stages:

1. **Breaking** balance This section describes the position Tori must first put Uke's body in to create the opportunity for the throw. Tori must set Uke up correctly for the throw.
2. **Grip** Where possible, Tori will use the traditional sleeve and lapel grip. For the description of the grip, I will assume that Tori is right-handed. For the traditional sleeve and lapel grip, Tori grips the lapel of Uke's jacket with her right hand and the sleeve of Uke's jacket with her left hand. If Tori wanted to use a left-handed grip, the roles of the hands are simply reversed. Tori would grab the lapel of Uke's jacket with her left hand and the sleeve of Uke's jacket with her right hand. It is important that at the start of each throw both Tori and Uke grip one another with the same grip. This is safer for both Tori and Uke and more realistic.
3. **Entry** This section describes the position Tori must put her body in to execute the throw correctly.
4. **Contact point** The purpose of any judo throw is to throw your opponent to the ground with the minimum of effort. In effect, Tori must use the whole of her body as a lever to execute the throw correctly. The correct point of contact between Tori and Uke's

bodies is therefore crucial to Tori's ability to use her body as a lever and throw Uke to the ground with the minimum of effort.
5. **Completion/finish** For a throw to be completed properly, Tori must throw Uke to the ground so that he lands on his back with force and velocity. To do this, Tori must keep control of Uke's body throughout the throw until Uke has landed on his back on the mat. If Tori loses control of Uke's body at any point during the throw, this provides Uke with an opportunity to escape, even if escape means Uke twisting his body just before he hits the mat so that he does not land on his back.
6. **Uke** If anyone wants to enjoy their judo and remain injury free, they must be able to fall correctly and without fear when they are thrown. When Tori practises a throw, it is important that Uke understands which breakfall he must perform. Performed correctly, the breakfall will allow Uke to fall safely and Tori to practise the throw properly. The description of each throw in this book will detail which breakfall Uke must perform when Tori throws him. It is important that Uke understands the role he will play in practice and how he can protect himself.

For the purposes of this book, Tori is a girl and Uke a boy. If I refer to 'she' or 'her', I am referring to Tori, if I refer to 'he' or 'him', I am referring to Uke. I hope this will help clarify the different roles of Tori and Uke in the description for each of the following throws. Also, Tori is dressed in a blue gi and Uke in a white gi for the photographs as this will help make it easier to identify them.

O Soto Gari (Major Outer Reaping)

O Soto Gari is one of the first throws that most judo players will learn. The reasons for this are that it is a relatively simple throw to learn and also a devastatingly effective throw when executed properly.

Common to all martial arts is a desire to move to the side of your opponent. This is because if you stand in front of your opponent square on, you provide your opponent with the largest possible target to attack. If you move to the side of your opponent, you make it much more difficult for your opponent to attack you. You are now a much smaller target and your opponent has a much more limited range of techniques that they can attack you with.

Moving to the side of your opponent is fundamental to executing O Soto Gari correctly. For most combat arts this would be seen as a defensive move, made either to avoid your opponent's attack or to make yourself a smaller target. In contrast, O Soto Gari is a throw that turns defence into attack. If you can move to the side of your opponent and break the balance of your opponent, then you will have created the opportunity to throw your opponent with O Soto Gari.

Breaking Balance

The most effective balance breaker for O Soto Gari is for Tori to move Uke to his right back corner (see Figure 17). Tori forces Uke backwards so that he has to balance his weight primarily on the heel of his right foot. His body is bent backwards and his head is over the right foot. To move Uke back and on to his right leg, Tori takes a diagonal step forward with her left foot. This diagonal step brings Tori to the side of Uke. Tori's left hand pulls Uke to his right, bringing Uke's weight over his right leg. It is important that Tori's left hand does not pull downwards as this will help Uke balance his weight on his right leg. Instead, Tori should pull slightly upwards with the left hand as this will help keep Uke on the heel of his right foot and therefore unbalanced. Tori uses her right hand to pull Uke close to her. This allows her to use the lever effect of her body that I described earlier. By pulling Uke close to her, Tori can use the whole of her body weight to drive Uke back and to the right as she takes her diagonal step forward.

Grip

The most common grip used for this throw is a traditional sleeve and lapel grip. It usually helps if Tori's right hand is fairly high on the lapel and in line with the collarbone of Uke. Tori's left hand should grip the right sleeve of Uke's jacket just above or on the elbow and on the seam of the jacket.

Entry

As I described above, the first step Tori takes is a diagonal step forward with her left leg, and this forward step should take Tori to the right side of Uke. This will put most of Tori's weight on to her front left leg so the left leg must be bent in order to keep Tori well balanced. Tori's right hand must control the position of Uke's head, so to maximize the strength of the right hand Tori keeps her right elbow pressed firmly against Uke's chest. The position of the right hand and elbow allows Tori to use the whole of the right side of her body to drive Uke's head in the direction of Tori's first step. At the same time, Tori uses her left hand to pull Uke's right sleeve in the same direction that Tori takes her first step forward. The hands therefore work together, with the right hand pushing and the left hand pulling. This combined action of the two hands working together coupled with Tori's first diagonal step brings Uke's head back over his right leg. In judo there is a saying: 'Where the head goes the body must follow.' By driving Uke's head backwards and to his right, Uke's weight has been shifted primarily back on to the heel of his right foot. Uke is now off balance, standing only on his right leg and balancing on the heel of his right foot.

Fig. 22 O Soto Gari.

Contact Point

Tori and Uke's chests should now be touching. The right side of Tori's chest should be in contact with the left side of Uke's chest. Tori's weight is primarily on her left leg and this allows her to lift her right leg off the ground and swing the right leg along the same diagonal line that her left leg followed. This brings the right leg of Tori around the outside and then up behind the right leg of Uke. When Tori swings the right leg through, it is vital that she keeps the right leg as close to Uke's body as possible. Tori's right leg is bent as it swings through, but once behind the body of Uke it should straighten and the toes point towards the floor. This straightening of the right leg and pointing of the toes is preparing the right leg to complete the throw. The right leg will perform what is called a reaping or sweeping action, and thus the right leg of Tori is often called the reaping or sweeping leg.

Completion

To complete the throw, Tori reaps (swings) the right leg backwards against the back of Uke's right leg. This movement takes Uke's right leg away from the floor and means that Uke can no longer stand up because Tori has swept away his only supporting leg. To maximize the power of Tori's reaping action, Tori bends her head forward as her leg reaps backwards and upwards. This means that her whole body provides the power for the reaping action of her right leg. Tori should finish the throw with her right leg in the air, her toes pointed and her head bowed forward close to the floor. The lower Tori can get her head and the higher she can get her right leg, the more power she will generate in the throw.

While Tori's reaping leg sweeps Uke's supporting leg away, Tori's upper body drives Uke's upper body back and down into the mat. Remember that Tori's chest is touching Uke's chest, so when Tori bends forward she drives Uke's upper body backwards. Tori has used her upper body and her hands to drive Uke's upper body backwards but has used the reaping action of her right leg to sweep Uke's legs away in the opposite direction. Tori has driven Uke's upper body downwards towards the floor while simultaneously driving Uke's legs up into the air with her right leg.

Uke

It is vital that Uke can perform Ushiro Ukemi (see Figure 7) properly when practising this throw. If Uke does not tuck his head in, then his head will hit the mat first when he is thrown. The speed of this throw can often catch Uke by surprise and it is vital that Uke has the necessary skill and confidence to stay safe and injury free with a properly executed Ushiro Ukemi. This is why it is so important that

Tori and Uke work together in practice. Tori must exercise the necessary control and skill required to allow Uke to breakfall correctly. It is only when Uke is confident with the breakfall that Tori should increase the power and speed of the throw.

Tai Otoshi (Body Drop)

Tai Otoshi means 'body drop' and is often regarded as an excellent technique for a lighter fighter against a heavier opponent. A good Tai Otoshi allows you to get underneath your opponent and throw an opponent forward with the minimum of effort and strength. Tai Otoshi is classified as a hand technique, and this is important because the hands are central to the successful execution of this throw. However, it is the placement of your feet and rotation of the hips that generate the power. The hands guide an opponent in the direction that they will fall, but it is the feet and hips that generate the power that propels an opponent through the air. As Tai Otoshi does not require you to lift your opponent high off the ground, your opponent's fall is very shallow. The result is that your opponent moves from the standing position to lying flat on the floor very quickly. Executed properly, it is a throw that usually takes your opponent by surprise and is very fast. Tai Otoshi is an excellent example of how you can use the superior strength, aggression and weight of an opponent to your advantage. Everything that your opponent would regard as an advantage is turned around and used against them. Your hands guide your opponent in the direction they are already moving in, your feet move your body out of the way so that your body does not block your opponent from the direction you want them to fall, and your hips accelerate the speed at which your opponent falls to the floor.

Breaking Balance

Tori wants Uke's weight to be moving forward and this can simply be achieved by Tori pulling Uke towards her. Any of the balance breakers that bring Uke forward and up on to his toes are ideal. However, in competition Tori wants to catch Uke by surprise so Tori wants to pull Uke forward towards her when Uke is not expecting an attack. Tori can actually start the attack from any direction that Uke might be moving in, so Uke may be moving backwards, forward or to the side before Tori pulls Uke forward and up on to his toes. If Tori can successfully do this, then it becomes very difficult for Uke to anticipate when he is being set up for the throw. As with all the throws in this book, it is important that Tai Otoshi is learnt in stages. When Tori and Uke first practise Tai Otoshi, Uke should be standing still, with his feet shoulder-width apart. Tori will simply break Uke's balance by pulling him forward and up on his toes. As Tori becomes more skilled, so the throw is practised on the move and so Tori develops the ability to pull Uke forward and up on to his toes whatever direction he may be moving in.

When Tori breaks Uke's balance by pulling him towards her, the pull from both the left and right hands should be equal. It is vital that Tori pulls Uke forward and up on to his toes because she wants to get underneath him. If she pulls downwards with her hands, then Uke is in a much better position from which to counter her attack. To offset any tendency to pull down with the left hand, Tori turns her left hand outwards as if she was looking at her wristwatch. This helps keeps the direction of the pull, with the left hand parallel to the floor. It also helps keep the left arm parallel to the floor. If the left elbow and wrist are basically in line, the arm is pulling in the direction Tori wants, but if the left elbow drops below the wrist then the pull on Uke's right arm will be downwards and far less effective.

Many judo players also roll their right hand inwards towards their chest as they pull Uke forward so that the palm of their hand is facing towards them. This small rotation of the wrist and hand helps pull their right arm in tight against the left side of Uke's body. Just as with the left arm, Tori wants the right elbow in line with the wrist, but this time the right elbow should be pointing down towards the floor. This is important because Tori will want to use her right arm to help with the rotational movement of the throw. It also prevents Tori from pulling Uke downwards and instead helps lift Uke up on to his toes.

Grip

For the purpose of this description, Tori is using a traditional, right-handed sleeve and lapel grip. However, Tai Otoshi can be done with a variety of different grips. What tends to vary is where Tori grips with her right hand; what tends not to vary is where Tori grips with her left hand. This is because the rotational pull of Tori's left hand on Uke's right sleeve is so important. At an advanced level, there are variations to the left-hand grip on Uke's right sleeve but this requires excellent technique. First develop good technique; when this goal has been achieved, only then should Tori start to vary where she grips with her left hand. To start with, Tori's left hand should always grip Uke's right sleeve just above the elbow and on the seam of the jacket.

Where Tori grips with her right hand on Uke's jacket is easier to vary. It is important for a beginner that they first learn how to do this throw with a lapel grip and this is the grip Tori uses in this description. However, a cross grip is also very effective. A cross grip is where Tori grips the right side of Uke's jacket with her right hand. So for a cross grip Tori would grip Uke's right lapel or the inside of Uke's right shoulder with her right hand. A cross grip is effective with Tai Otoshi because it emphasizes the rotational movement of Tori's body that is so important to the execution this throw. It should be remembered that a cross grip in competition can only be held for 3 seconds: Tori must throw Uke within this 3-second window or she will be penalized.

Entry

Tori steps forward with her right foot as she pulls Uke towards her. Tori places her right foot at approximately the midpoint between Uke's feet. Tori keeps the toes of the right foot pointed so that she is standing on the ball of her right foot. Tori pivots on her right foot and turns the left side of her body away from Uke in an anticlockwise direction. Tori's left leg swings around so that her left foot lands is line with the right foot. Tori's body is now facing away from Uke and her stance is strong. With her feet in line and slightly wider than shoulder-width apart, her weight is evenly distributed between her feet. In effect, Tori has turned her body through 180 degrees. She started the throw looking at Uke but has finished the entry to this throw by turning around and looking in the opposite direction, directly away from Uke.

As Tori turns in for the throw, it is important that she maintains the pull from both her left and right hands. As she gets closer to Uke and turns, so Tori's left arm must bend to accommodate the change in the position of her body. The left arm must stay parallel with the floor so that the left elbow and wrist are in line. Tori must also bend the right arm as she turns in for the throw. Tori wants to bend her right arm so that the elbow points down to the floor. This means that Tori can bring her right arm in tight against the left side of Uke's body.

Contact Point

It is important that Tori has her back to Uke but that her body is not blocking Uke from falling forward. Tori should therefore be able to look over her right shoulder and see most of Uke's body. Tori's right arm is bent and the forearm resting against the left side of Uke's chest. The back of Tori's right buttock should be in front and touching the front of Uke's left hip. Tori should have a grip of Uke's right arm just above the elbow with her left hand. Tori then extends her right leg across Uke's body so that the back of Tori's calf is touching Uke's right shin. It is important that the right foot passes across in front of Uke's right foot but not so far across that Tori has to move her body across to the right and therefore block Uke from falling forward. Tori's left leg is bent so that she is lower to the ground

Fig. 23 Tai Otoshi.

than Uke. This is important because it means that Tori's centre of gravity is lower than Uke's. This helps Tori maintain control of Uke's body since being lower than Uke helps Tori to keep Uke moving forward and up on his toes. It is very important that, at this stage, Tori's weight is evenly distributed between right and left legs so that she has a strong, stable base. This is important because without a strong and stable base Tori cannot turn her hips from right to left. It is this twisting movement of the hips that produces the rotational force that it is necessary to execute the throw properly.

Completion

To complete the throw, Tori pivots on both her feet in an anticlockwise direction. Tori is turning from her right to her left. As she turns, the left hand of Tori pulls and the right hand of Tori pushes Uke around. This pull and pushing movement of Tori's hands is vital because it pulls Uke forward and around Tori's right hip. The pull and push of

Tori's hands also helps Tori to turn her body from right to left. If Tori is smaller than Uke, then Tori will also drive the right hand upwards. This helps Tori to get underneath Uke and keep Uke off balance. This is why Tai Otoshi is such an effective throw for the smaller player on a taller opponent.

The rotational force generated by the push and pulling movement of Tori's hands and the turn of her body away from Uke, brings Uke up and over Tori's extended right leg, effectively tripping Uke as he falls forward. To regain his balance, Uke needs to step forward with his right leg but he can not because Tori's right leg is blocking his right leg from coming forward. The left turn that Tori makes with her body pulls Uke forward over her right leg. The turn is important and powerful because it enables Tori to use the whole of her body weight to throw Uke forward. This turn to the left by Tori does not end until her head is in line with her left knee. The position of the feet has not changed but most of her weight is now on her left leg. The left foot is therefore flat on the floor but the left knee is bent almost at right angles. The right leg is also bent but Tori's right foot is up on her toes. Tori has effectively turned her body through 90 degrees to complete the throw. As Uke falls to the ground, Tori must maintain a strong pull on Uke's right sleeve with her left hand. This helps pull Uke around so that he falls on to his back rather than his side. It is also important that as Tori turns her body to her left, she keeps a straight back and does not bend forward as this will reduce the rotational force generated by turning her body.

Uke

It is important that Uke is comfortable with both Ushiro and Yoko Ukemi. Ideally, Tori wants to land Uke on his back, in which case Uke will need to breakfall with Ushiro Ukemi. With Ushiro Ukemi, it is always important that Uke keeps his head tucked in to protect it. However, if Tori loses control of Uke during the throw, Uke may well land on his side, in which case he will need to breakfall with Yoko Ukemi. Again, it is important that Uke keeps his head tucked in and that he does not try to put his left arm out to help break his fall as this will make the left shoulder vulnerable to injury.

With Tai Otoshi, Uke moves from the standing position to lying flat on the floor very quickly. Therefore, to begin with it is important that Uke is prepared for Tori's attack and has time to breakfall safely. It is only when Tori and Uke have practised Tai Otoshi together and both are confident and competent, that this throw should be practised with speed and on the move. If Tori were to take Uke by surprise or execute Tai Otoshi very quickly, a relatively inexperienced Uke would not have the skills to breakfall properly or safely.

O Goshi (Hip Throw)

O Goshi is one of the first throws a judo player will learn. O Goshi essentially means major hip throw and, as the name suggests, it is the hip that is the centre point of the throw. There are several different hip throws, such as Harai Goshi (sweeping hip throw) and Hane Goshi (springing hip throw), and each of these techniques uses the hip as the centre point of the throw. However, O Goshi is the simplest hip throw to execute technically. The foot movements required to execute O Goshi correctly are also similar to many other judo throws, such as the Seoi Nage throws (shoulder throws). If a judo player can learn to perform O Goshi well, it is likely that they will also have the basic skills and technique required for many of the other judo throws that they will inevitably go on to learn as their judo develops.

As the hip is so important to this throw, where Tori places her pelvis in relation to Uke's hips is central to executing it correctly. The principle of the throw is relatively simple: if Tori's hips are lower than Uke's hips, Tori can then bring Uke forward over her hips with the minimum of effort. If Tori's hips are higher than Uke's hips, Tori's hips will actually block Uke from falling forward and Tori would have to lift Uke up on to her hips and then throw him. This would require considerable strength and a fairly helpful Uke. It is the height of Tori's hips in comparison to Uke's hips that is the key to this throw.

Breaking Balance

Tori needs Uke's weight to be moving forward so any of the balance breakers that bring Uke forward and up on to his toes are ideal. It is important for Tori to try to bring Uke up on to his toes because Tori will want to get her hips lower than Uke's hips once she has turned in for the throw. So the higher Uke is up on his toes, the easier it is for Tori to turn in and get her hips lower than those of Uke. It is Uke's forward movement that will provide the momentum for O Goshi. The throw requires relatively little effort to execute because Tori uses the momentum Uke has generated by moving forward towards her to throw Uke. In fact, the faster Tori can get Uke to move towards her, the more momentum is generated and the easier the throw becomes for Tori to execute.

Grip

The basic grip for O Goshi changes during the throw. Tori starts the throw with a traditional, right-handed sleeve and lapel grip. So Tori's right hand grips Uke's left lapel and Tori's left hand grips Uke's right sleeve just above the elbow. Tori uses this grip to break Uke's balance and bring

him forward and up on to his toes. As Tori turns in for the throw, she releases her right hand from gripping Uke's left lapel and places her right arm around Uke's waist. With this grip, Tori will bring Uke forward and over her right hip. As Uke falls to the floor, Tori will let go of Uke's waist with her right arm but keep a strong grip of Uke's right sleeve with her left hand. This allows Tori to keep control of Uke's body as he falls to the floor.

Tori can vary how high up on Uke's back she puts her right arm when she turns in. If Tori is taller than Uke, she will probably put her arm around Uke higher up on his back rather than around the waist. If Tori is the same height or shorter than Uke, it is more likely that Tori will put her arm around Uke's waist. However, if Tori's right arm comes up and around Uke's shoulders, so that Tori's right arm is now higher that Uke's left shoulder, then the throw becomes Tsuri Komi Goshi. Whatever height Tori's right arm is in relation to Uke, the principles of the throw remain the same.

Entry

The entry into O Goshi is simple but must be precise. Tori steps across the front of Uke with her right foot, placing the right foot in front but just inside the line of Uke's right foot. Tori keeps the toes pointed so that she is standing on the ball of her right foot. Her weight is evenly distributed between her feet. At this stage of the throw, Tori moves her right arm to around Uke's waist, the right side of her body is facing Uke and her right foot is almost in line with Uke's right foot. Tori then turns on the ball of the right foot, allowing her to bring her left leg around and into line with her right leg so that she now has her back to Uke. Tori has performed a 180-degree turn and has gone from facing Uke to facing away from Uke. Tori's feet should be about shoulder-width apart but slightly narrower than Uke's feet. Both Tori and Uke's feet should be facing in exactly the same direction.

This entry into O Goshi is usually called the 'two step'. The two-step entry is important in judo and should be practised again and again. The movement of Tori, from stepping across Uke's body to rotating in so that Tori is facing away from Uke, should be smooth and quick. Speed will only come with practice; try not to sacrifice good technique in search of speed. Speed of movement should only come from proper practice and the application of good technique – do not force it.

Contact

Tori is now facing away from Uke. Her feet are pointing in the same direction but are slightly narrower than those of Uke. Tori's hips are lower than Uke's and this is vital to the correct execution of this throw. A good marker for this is

Fig. 24 O Goshi.

if Tori's belt is lower than Uke's belt; this simple point helps Tori visualize how high her hips need to be in relation to Uke. To get the correct height for her hips, Tori will usually have to bend her legs. The degree that she has to bend her legs will depend on the height of Uke. The shorter Uke is in relation to Tori, the more Tori must bend her legs to get her hips lower than Uke's hips. Tori must always have some bend in the legs because this throw cannot be done with straight legs. Tori will want to generate some upwards lift during the throw and this can only be done if the legs are bent at the knees on entry into the throw. Also, by bending her legs Tori has a stronger base and therefore better balance.

The back of Tori's pelvis is against the front of Uke's pelvis. Tori's hips are in line with Uke's hips. In some cases, Tori can have her hips slightly further across the front of Uke, so that her right hip is further to the right than Uke's right hip. Tori's back is against Uke's stomach and chest. If Tori and Uke are a similar height, Tori's right shoulder blade should be touching Uke's chest. Tori's right arm is wrapped around Uke's waist and Tori has a strong grip of Uke's right sleeve with her left hand.

Completion

It is important to remember that by breaking Uke's balance to the front (see Figure 14), Uke is moving forward towards Tori. By stepping across Uke and turning 180 degrees, Tori has blocked Uke from moving any further forward. However, when Tori blocks Uke from moving forward she only blocks his legs from moving forward; with her hands and upper body she helps the top half of Uke's body to keep moving forward. Uke's legs are stuck where they are but his body from the waist up is still moving forward. Uke simply falls forward over Tori's right hip. Tori has used her hips like a trip wire and allowed or helped Uke simply to fall over her right hip.

Tori's left hand pulls Uke forward. It is important that the left hand pulls slightly upwards and not down as it is important to keep Uke up on his toes. Tori's right arm also brings Uke forward but her right arm is behind Uke, so Tori's right arm effectively pushes Uke forward as her left arm pulls him forward. As Uke cannot step forward, because Tori is in the way, Uke is drawn on to Tori's right hip.

Tori now straightens her legs, and because her hips are lower than Uke's, Uke's feet are lifted from the ground. Uke has no base or balance because his feet are no longer in contact with the floor. This is why it is so important that on the entry to O Goshi Tori keeps her legs bent. Without bending her legs she cannot then get this important lifting action. By keeping her centre of gravity lower than Uke's, Tori can use Uke's forward momentum to draw him on to her right hip; by straightening her legs she then can accelerate Uke's forward momentum over her right hip. Tori's hands and arms help complete the throw by keeping Uke's upper body moving forward.

As Uke falls forward over Tori's right hip, Tori bends forward and turns her head to the left. By bending forward Tori is continuing to bring Uke forward and over her right hip. By turning her head to the left Tori increases the effective pull of her left hand and push of her right arm on Uke. The left turn of the head also effectively drops Tori's right shoulder closer to the floor and helps creates the space for Uke to fall into. The less resistance there is from Tori's body and the more Tori can encourage Uke's body to fall forward over her right hip, the more effective the throw is.

Tori brings Uke around flat on to his back on the mat with a strong pull on Uke's right arm with her left hand. Tori should never let go of Uke's sleeve when she throws him. The pull of her left arm is essential if Tori is to keep control of Uke's body and land him on his back. This is vital if Tori is to score an Ippon, maximum points in a competition. However, in practice it is also important that Tori keeps control of Uke's body from a safety point of view. By pulling Uke around and on to his back, Tori is helping pull Uke's body in to the correct position for the breakfall, in this case Ushiro Ukemi. By helping Uke to breakfall correctly Tori is reducing the risk of injury to Uke. On completion of O Goshi, Tori should still have hold of Uke's left sleeve, her back should be straight, her feet shoulder-width apart and her legs slightly bent.

Uke

The breakfall Uke needs to use for O Goshi is Mae Mawarai Ukemi. The path Uke's body follows when he is thrown with O Goshi is almost identical to the path his body follows when he practises Mae Mawari Ukemi. This is where the hours of practice for Mae Mawari Ukemi pay off for Uke. If Uke has practised his Mae Mawari Ukemi, he should have little difficulty with Tori throwing him with O Goshi. The important principles to adhere to are that the head is tucked in and does not touch the mat. It is the back of Uke's shoulders that must first make contact with the mat. A good Tori will have the skill to pull Uke into the correct position to breakfall correctly, making life easier and safer for Uke. However, a good Uke should never rely on Tori to get it right and, as a novice, Tori may struggle to execute the throw correctly. Uke must look after himself and ensure that he does not land on his head or his shoulder. He does that by tucking his head in, rolling over Tori's hip with the throw and making contact with the mat with the back of his right shoulder first.

Uki Goshi (Floating Hip Throw)

It is difficult for the untrained observer to see any differences in the execution of O Goshi and Uki Goshi. However, there are important differences between these two throws that any good judo player should understand. O Goshi is often referred to as a full hip throw and Uki Goshi as a half hip throw. This description does not fully explain the differences between the two throws but does help highlight the importance of hip alignment or placement. For O Goshi, Tori's hips are literally directly in front of Uke's hips and facing in exactly the same direction. With Uki Goshi, Tori's right hip must be inside the line of Uke's right hip (see Figure 25).

With O Goshi, Tori will push her right hip through until the hip is in line with Uke's right hip. Tori will then straighten her legs, lift Uke from the ground and throw him forward over her right hip. Uke should land on his back in front of Tori. In contrast, with Uki Goshi, Tori will not push her right hip through; instead, Tori's right hip will be inside the line of Uke's right hip. Tori will still bring Uke forward on to her right hip, but she will not straighten her legs to the same degree to lift Uke from the ground. Instead, Tori will use her hips to drive Uke upwards.

With O Goshi, Uke falls forward over Tori's right hip and lands on his back in front of Tori. With Uki Goshi, Uke pivots around Tori's right hip and lands on his back to the right side of Tori. When executed properly, Uki Goshi is the faster technique because there is less lifting action to Uki Goshi. Uke is not loaded up on to Tori's hip; instead, Uke is drawn up tight against Tori's right hip and Tori uses the driving and twisting action of her hips to throw Uke. Uki Goshi therefore relies on a higher level of skill than O Goshi but is a throw that can be used more easily against a heavier opponent.

O Goshi is one of the first judo throws that most judo players will learn and it is a throw that most players learn without too much difficulty. Uki Goshi is not so easy to learn and judo players can often get confused between the two throws. I would therefore recommend that you learn O Goshi first before you learn Uki Goshi. Learn O Goshi well and then the additional skills necessary for Uki Goshi can naturally be developed from the good basic skills that were learnt with O Goshi. If you try to learn these two throws at the same time, the result will be a very confused judo player who can not perform either throw very well.

Uki Goshi is reputed to have been one of Jigaro Kano's favourite throws. The speed of the throw in comparison with O Goshi probably makes it a more effective throw in competition. It is a throw that any good judo player should spend time on learning and developing.

Breaking Balance

Tori needs Uke's weight to be moving forward so any of the balance breakers that bring Uke forward and up on to his toes are ideal. Again, it is important for Tori to try to bring Uke up on to his toes because Tori will want to get her hips lower than Uke's hips once she has turned in for the throw. When Tori and Uke first practise Uki Goshi, it is easiest to begin with if Uke is standing still, with his feet shoulder-width apart. Tori can simply break Uke's balance by pulling him forward and up on to his toes. However, as soon as Tori is capable, the throw should be practised on the move. Once again, it is Uke's forward movement that will provide the momentum for Uki Goshi. The throw requires relatively little effort to execute because Tori uses the momentum Uke has generated, by moving forward towards her, to throw him.

Grip

As with O Goshi, the basic grip for Uki Goshi changes during the throw. Tori starts the throw with a traditional, right-handed sleeve and lapel grip. Tori uses this grip to break Uke's balance and bring him forward and up on to his toes. As Tori turns in for the throw, Tori releases her right hand from gripping Uke's left lapel and places her right arm around Uke's waist. With this grip, Tori will bring Uke forward tight against her hip. Tori then uses the drive from her hips to throw Uke. As Uke falls to the floor, Tori will let go of Uke's waist with her right arm but keep a strong grip of Uke's right sleeve with her left arm. This allows Tori to keep control of Uke's body as he falls to the floor.

Tori can vary how high up on Uke's back she puts her right arm when she turns in. If Tori is the same height or shorter than Uke, then Tori will put her arm around Uke's waist. If Tori is taller than Uke, she will probably put her arm around Uke higher up on his back. Whatever height Tori's right arm is in relation to Uke, the principles of the throw remain the same.

Entry

Tori steps across the front of Uke with her right leg, placing her right foot just inside the line of Uke's right foot. Tori keeps the toes of her right foot pointed so that she is standing on the ball of her foot. Her weight is evenly distributed between her feet. It is at this stage of the throw that Tori moves her right arm to around Uke's waist. The right side of her body is now facing Uke and her right foot is inside the line of Uke's right foot.

Tori then turns on the ball of her right foot and this allows her to bring her left leg around and into line with her right leg so that she now has her back to Uke. Tori has performed a 180-degree turn and has gone from facing Uke to facing away from Uke. It is important that both of Tori's feet are inside the line of Uke's feet and that both Tori and Uke's feet are facing in the same direction.

The entry into Uki Goshi is the same two steps used for O Goshi. The important difference with Uki Goshi is that with her first step Tori has not stepped so far across Uke with her right foot. Again, this two-step entry should be smooth and quick, so practice is important. Speed will only come with practice but do not sacrifice good technique in search of speed.

Contact

Tori is now facing away from Uke. Her feet are pointing in the same direction but are slightly closer together than those of Uke. Tori's hips should be lower than Uke's and Tori will usually have to bend her legs to achieve this. The degree to which Tori has to bend her legs will depend on the height of Uke. The shorter Uke is in relation to Tori, the more Tori must bend her legs; the taller Uke is in relation to Tori, then the less Tori will have to bend her legs. However, Tori should always have some bend in the legs because this throw cannot be done with straight legs. Tori

Fig. 25 Uki Goshi.

will want to generate some upwards lift during the throw and this can only be done if the legs are bent at the knees on entry into the throw. With O Goshi, the more Tori bends her legs the greater the upward lift generated for the throw. With Uki Goshi, this upward lift is of less importance so the degree to which Tori has to bend her legs is also less important. It is best to have a relatively smaller bend in the knees than in O Goshi, but is still vital that Tori's hips are slightly lower than Uke's hips.

The back of Tori's pelvis is against the front of Uke's pelvis. However, in contrast to O Goshi, Tori's hips are not in line with Uke's hips. Instead, Tori's right hip is inside the line of Uke's right hip and Tori's left hip is outside the line of Uke's left hip. Tori's back is against Uke's stomach and chest. If Tori and Uke are a similar height, Tori's right shoulder blade should be touching Uke's chest. Tori's right arm is wrapped around Uke's waist and Tori has a strong grip of Uke's right sleeve with her left hand.

Completion

By breaking Uke's balance to the front (see Figure 14), Uke is moving forward towards Tori. It is important that Tori keeps Uke moving forward so Tori's left hand maintains a strong pull on Uke's right sleeve. The left hand pulls slightly upwards and not down as it is important to keep Uke up on his toes. Tori's right arm also brings Uke forward but her right arm is behind Uke, so Tori's right arm effectively pushes Uke forward as her left arm pulls him forward.

Tori now straightens her legs and drives her right hip up and into the inside of Uke's pelvis. Tori's hips are lower than Uke's so Uke's feet are lifted from the ground by Tori straightening her legs. However, this lifting action is not as powerful as in O Goshi and the drive upwards is more limited and does not take Uke so high. Instead, the drive from Tori's right hip also pushes Uke's hips upwards and helps keep Uke's feet off the floor. Tori has used Uke's forward momentum to draw him up against her right hip, and by then straightening her legs and driving with her own hips she accelerates Uke's forward momentum around her right hip.

As Uke falls forward and around Tori's right hip, Tori bends forward and turns her head to the left. By bending forward, Tori is continuing to drive Uke forward and around her right hip. By turning her head to the left, Tori increases the effective pull of her left hand and push of her right arm on Uke's upper body. The left turn of the head also effectively drops Tori's right shoulder closer to the floor and helps creates the space for Uke to fall into. Tori brings Uke around flat on to his back on the mat with a strong pull on Uke's right arm with her left hand. Tori should never let go of Uke when she throws him. The pull of her left arm is essential if Tori is to keep control of Uke's body and land him on his back. On completion of Uki Goshi, Tori should still have hold of Uke's left sleeve, her back should be straight, her feet shoulder-width apart and her legs slightly bent.

Uke

With O Goshi, Uke rolls forward over Tori's right hip and lands in front of Tori, while with Uki Goshi Uke is twisted around in the air and lands at the side of Tori. If the throw is done correctly, Uke will still need to execute Mae Mawarai Ukemi but he will have less time to execute the breakfall than he did with O Goshi because Uki Goshi is a much faster throw. It therefore usually helps if a novice Tori is partnered at first with an experienced Uke because an experienced Uke should have better breakfall skills to cope with the faster fall. With Mae Mawarai Ukemi, Uke must make sure that he tucks his head in and makes contact with the mat with the back of his right shoulder first. However, because Uke falls to the right side

of Tori and not in front of her, Uke may have to breakfall with Yoko Ukemi instead. It is important that Uke understands that he may have to adjust and change his breakfall if Tori loses control of the throw. Uki Goshi requires a higher level of skill from Tori than O Goshi so there is a greater chance that Tori may lose control of Uke during the throw.

Harai Goshi (Sweeping Hip Throw)

There is a popular story that Jigaro Kano was able to constantly get the better of one of his top students in practice with Uki Goshi (*see above*). The student became frustrated at Jigaro Kano's ability always to beat him with this throw so he developed an escape. Whenever Jigaro Kano turned in to throw him, the student would take a diagonal step forward with his right foot. This meant that Jigaro Kano did not have enough contact with his hips to lift the student from the ground and throw him. By taking this diagonal step forward the student could keep one leg firmly planted on the ground and twist out of the throw. Jigaro Kano became frustrated that his student could now escape from one of his favourite throws. So, in turn, he developed Uki Goshi into Harai Goshi so that he could stop his student from escaping. To escape, his student had to commit most of his weight on to the leg he stepped forward with; Jigaro Kano's solution to this was simple: sweep this leg away and his student could no longer twist out of the throw.

This story illustrates two very important points. The first is that judo is always evolving and changing as a martial art and a sport. As judo players work out a counter or an escape to one technique, so they will develop another technique to defeat and frustrate their opponent. This is why judo will always continue to evolve and change with time. The second point is that while Harai Goshi is a hip throw and therefore similar in design to Uki Goshi, there are some fundamental and important differences between the two throws. I recommend that any student should learn Uki Goshi first because Uki Goshi requires the basic skills that are also essential for learning Harai Goshi. Harai Goshi is a more complex throw and will therefore require additional skills. Try to learn the two throws at the same time and it is likely that a student will become confused and struggle to learn either throw properly.

If Tori can execute Uki Goshi correctly, she will already have the basic skills with which to set Harai Goshi up correctly. The mistake that most students will then make is that they will try to both lift and sweep Uke over their hips. If Tori can bring Uke forward on to her hips and then lift him from the ground, there is no need to sweep, and

Tori should complete what is essentially an Uki Goshi throw. It is very easy for beginners to confuse the skills they need for Uki Goshi with the skills that they need for Harai Goshi. Tori should set the throw up as if she is going to throw Uke with Uki Goshi, but just before Tori commits to completing the throw, Uke should take that diagonal step forward. Tori can no longer get the lifting action she wants to complete Uki Goshi and she must now sweep to throw Uke. It is a great way to learn Harai Goshi for the first time because it highlights the differences between Harai Goshi and Uki Goshi and helps Tori focus on the new set of skills that she must learn to execute the throw properly. It is also a great example of how Tori and Uke can work together and help one another learn and develop better judo skills.

Breaking Balance

For all hip throws, Tori wants to bring Uke forward and ideally up on to his toes. Uke's forward movement provides momentum to any hip throw and reduces the need for Tori to use power or strength to execute the throw correctly. Bringing Uke up on to his toes raises his centre of gravity and makes him more vulnerable to being thrown. When learning any throw, it is important to get into the practice of breaking the balance correctly right from the start. This can sometimes be forgotten with a cooperative Uke. Uke stands still and lets Tori throw him because Tori is beginning to learn the throw and needs to concentrate on perfecting the correct sequence of movements that make up Harai Goshi. Tori can forget that Uke is effectively helping her and that getting Uke in the correct position to throw will be a lot more difficult if Uke resists or is on the move. If she is not careful, Tori can start to focus more on the technical movements required to throw Uke than on breaking Uke's balance and setting the throw up correctly. This is a mistake. Breaking Uke's balance and bringing Uke up and forward is essential if Tori is going to throw Uke.

When you practise a throw over and over again, you must practise exactly what you need to do under pressure or in competition. What you practise must be what you would do. It is really important, therefore, that as Tori becomes better at Harai Goshi, her practice should develop and reflect the reality of competition as much as possible. Uke should become less helpful as it is essential that Tori develops her ability to execute the throw on the move. To be able to use Harai Goshi on the move, it is important that Tori develops the ability to pull Uke forward on to his toes whatever direction he may be moving in.

Grip

The basic grip for O Goshi, Uki Goshi and Harai Goshi is the same to begin with and changes during the throw. Tori starts the throw with a traditional, right-handed sleeve and lapel grip. Tori uses this grip to break Uke's balance and bring him forward and up on to his toes. As Tori turns in for the throw, she releases her right hand from gripping Uke's left lapel and places her right arm around Uke's waist. With this grip, Tori will bring Uke forward and up close to her body. As Tori sweeps Uke over her hip, she will let go of Uke's waist with her right arm but keep a strong grip of Uke's right sleeve with her left arm. This allows Tori to keep control of Uke's body throughout the throw and helps her pull Uke around on to his back.

Harai Goshi can be done from a variety of different grips. Tori can use the traditional sleeve and lapel grip throughout the throw and does not have to grip Uke around the waist. Tori can use a traditional collar and sleeve grip or a cross grip, where she again grips the sleeve, but grips Uke's right lapel instead of his left lapel. Whichever grip Tori uses, the principles of the throw remain the same. As a student becomes more proficient with Harai Goshi, I would encourage them to try a variety of different grips. By varying the grip, a judo player can disguise which throw they are going to attempt. In competition, judo players do not always get the grip that they want, so if you can practise a throw from a variety of different grips, you then increase the opportunities or situations from which you can perform the throw. The fact that you can use Harai Goshi from a number of different grips makes this throw a very useful tool in any judo player's repertoire of skills.

For beginners, it is best to use a traditional sleeve and lapel grip that changes during the throw because this gives Tori the best control of Uke's body during the throw. This makes practice safer and helps Tori drill and learn the skills necessary to execute this throw correctly. It is only once Tori has mastered Harai Goshi from this traditional grip that she should then go on to develop her skills with different grips. Get the basics right first.

Entry

The entry into Harai Goshi is very similar to Uki Goshi. Tori steps across the front of Uke with her right foot, placing the right foot just inside the line of Uke's right foot. Tori keeps the toes pointed so that she is standing on the ball of her right foot. Her weight is evenly distributed between her feet. At this stage of the throw, Tori changes her grip so that she can put her right arm around Uke's waist, the right side of her body facing Uke. Tori then turns on the ball of the right foot, allowing her to bring her left leg around and into line with her right leg so that she now has her back to Uke. Tori has performed a 180-degree turn and has gone from facing Uke to facing away from Uke.

Tori should keep a strong pull on Uke's right sleeve with her left hand. Tori's left arm should be bent and almost parallel with the floor. This is important because an upward pull keeps Uke off balance and helps draw Uke close to Tori's body. Any downward pull by the left arm would help Uke plant his weight firmly back on his feet and stop the momentum of the throw. By pulling upwards with the left arm, Tori not only brings Uke forward but also gets him to commit most of his weight on to his right leg, the leg Tori wants to sweep. Tori's right arm (wrapped around Uke's waist) pulls Uke close to Tori's body and then keeps him there. This strong right-arm grip around Uke's waist prevents him from shifting his weight backwards and avoiding the throw.

Contact

Tori, is now facing away from Uke. The back of Tori's pelvis is against the front of Uke's pelvis. It is important that Tori has not got her hips too far across in front of Uke's hips. For both Uki Goshi and Harai Goshi, it is important that

Fig. 26 Harai Goshi.

Tori's right hip is inside the line of Uke's right hip and not outside. Tori's back is against Uke's stomach and chest. Tori's right arm is wrapped around Uke's waist and Tori has a strong grip of Uke's right sleeve with her left hand. The left arm is bent and the elbow pointing upwards so that the left arm is almost parallel with the ground. Instead of standing firmly with her weight evenly distributed between her feet, Tori puts most of her weight on to her left leg. This allows her to point the toes of her right foot and therefore prepare her right leg for the sweeping action that must follow to complete the throw. Tori's pointed toes should be touching the mat just outside the line of Uke's right foot. This means that Tori's right foot is outside the line of Uke's right foot but her right hip is inside the line of Uke's right hip. Tori's right leg, therefore, lies diagonally across the front of Uke's right leg.

Completion

Tori sweeps her right leg backwards, effectively sweeping Uke's right leg away from underneath him. In sweeping her leg back, Tori brings her head forward; this forward movement is often referred to as 'bowing to the mat'. By sweeping her right leg backwards, Tori has swept Uke up and over her right hip; by bowing forward to the mat, Tori also uses her upper body to keep Uke falling forward over her hip. As Tori bows her head forward to the mat and Uke falls forward over her hip, Tori also drops her right shoulder down towards the mat. This rotational movement of the shoulders is exaggerated by Tori turning her head to the left. By dropping her right shoulder downwards, Tori accelerates Uke's fall forward. As Uke falls forward, Tori must keep a strong grip and pull with her left hand on Uke's right sleeve. The combination of Tori dropping her right shoulder downwards and pulling with her left hand on Uke's right sleeve produces a rotational force on Uke that should bring him around on to his back as he lands on the mat.

Uke

With the hip throws, Uke will need to execute Mae Mawarai Ukemi. It is important that Uke tucks his head in when he is thrown. For beginners, it is sometimes difficult to understand that although you are being thrown forward, Tori will still land you with force on your back. As a result, many beginners do not tuck their head in when they are thrown with Harai Goshi. The force of being thrown on to their back surprises them and their head is thrown backwards so that they bang the back of their head on the mat. When performed correctly, Harai Goshi is a very powerful throw and Uke can find himself hitting the mat much faster and harder than he anticipated. Protect the head and tuck it in. As with all well-structured practice, Tori should start slowly and sensibly. Tori should only add speed and power to the throw as she improves. This should mean that Tori always has the right level of control in practice to throw Uke correctly and Uke has the skills and time to protect himself with a proper break-fall.

Ippon Seoi Nage (One-Arm Shoulder Throw)

A judo throw that involves lifting your opponent off the ground and throwing them over your shoulder is referred to as a Seoi Nage, a shoulder throw. However, a throw that involves dropping to the ground and pulling your opponent over your shoulder is referred to as a Seoi Otoshi, a shoulder drop. Seoi Nage and Seoi Otoshi are two of the most common throws used in judo competition.

Due to the popularity of the shoulder throw, there are many variations to Seoi Nage. Most of these variations are based on differences in how Tori grips Uke's judo gi. Ippon Seoi Nage uses a one-handed grip whereas Morote Seoi Nage uses a two-handed grip. Both Morote Seoi Nage and Eri Seoi Nage use a two-handed grip, but the two-handed grip for Morote Seoi Nage is different from that of Eri Seoi Nage. Morote Seoi Nage starts with the traditional sleeve and lapel grip while Eri Seoi Nage starts with Tori gripping the sleeve and lapel of Uke's gi on the same side.

Whichever Seoi Nage Tori attempts, the fundamental principles of the throw remain the same. The purpose of the throw is to get underneath Uke and to help him fall forward over Tori's shoulder. As with O Goshi, it is important that Tori gets her hips lower than Uke's hips so she can bring Uke forward over her shoulder with the minimum of effort. This often means that Seoi Nage is seen as an ideal throw for the shorter judo player against the taller player. It is true that the shorter you are in comparison to your opponent, the easier it is to get your hips lower than those of your opponent. However, a good Seoi Nage gives you excellent control of your opponent's body and done well it is a devastatingly effective throw. It is therefore a throw every good judo player should practise and develop.

Probably the most common shoulder throw is Ippon Seoi Nage, which means 'one point shoulder throw'. Ippon Seoi Nage is usually one of the first throws a judo player will learn. It is from learning Ippon Seoi Nage that most judo players will then go on to learn and develop variations to the Seoi Nage throw. It is Ippon Seoi Nage that we are going to look at here and I would strongly recommend that you master it first before moving on and trying to learn other variations of the Seoi Nage throw. The fundamental principles of Ippon Seoi Nage will be the same as any other Seoi Nage throw, so learn the funda-

mentals of Ippon Seoi Nage well and it will be much easier to go on and learn the different Seoi Nage throws.

Breaking Balance

Tori needs Uke's weight to be moving forward so any of the balance breakers that bring Uke forward and up on to his toes are ideal. It is important for Tori to bring Uke up on to his toes because Tori will want to get her hips lower than Uke's hips once she has turned in for the throw. The higher Uke is up on his toes, the easier it is for Tori to turn in and get her hips lower than Uke's hips. When Tori and Uke first practise Ippon Seoi Nage, Uke should be standing still with his feet shoulder-width apart. Tori will simply break Uke's balance by pulling him forward and up on to his toes. However, as Tori becomes more skilled, it is vital that she practises Ippon Seoi Nage on the move. The shoulder throws rely on exactly the same balance-breaking principles that the hip throws do because it is Uke's forward movement that will provide the momentum for the throw. Ippon Seoi Nage requires relatively little effort to execute because Tori uses the momentum Uke has generated by moving forward towards her to throw Uke. It does not matter if it is a hip or shoulder throw; the faster Tori can get Uke to move towards her, the more momentum is generated and the easier the throw becomes for Tori to execute.

Grip

As with all Seoi Nage throws, it is the grip for Ippon Seoi Nage that defines this throw and differentiates it from other Seoi Nage throws. As with O Goshi, Tori will need to change her grip during the throw. The throw starts with a right-handed, traditional sleeve and lapel grip. Tori will step forward with her right foot and release her right hand from the grip she has on Uke's left lapel. As Tori turns in for the throw, she passes her right arm underneath the right arm of Uke. Tori places the inside of her right elbow underneath Uke's right arm and up against the top of Uke's right tricep. Tori then bends her right arm so that her right hand is pointing towards the ceiling. In effect, Tori has clamped Uke's right arm with her right arm and Tori now has a grip of Uke's right arm with both her left hand and right arm. It is very important that Tori's right arm is bent and grips the top of Uke's tricep. If Tori does not clamp Uke's arm properly, then Uke's right arm can slip over Tori's right shoulder and around Tori's neck. This makes it very difficult for Tori to execute the throw properly and leaves Tori vulnerable to a choke or strangle from Uke. It is therefore vital that Tori clamps Uke's right arm between her bicep and forearm, like a vice.

A helpful tip for making this change of grip easier is to turn the left hand outwards as if you were trying to look at your wristwatch. When Tori steps forward with the right foot, she turns her left hand so the palm of her hand is facing away from her. This pulls Uke's right arm away from his body and up towards the ceiling. This action creates a larger gap between Uke's right arm and body through which Tori can now put her right arm. If Uke's right upper arm lies against his chest, Tori cannot get her right arm underneath Uke's right arm and get the grip she needs to execute the throw correctly. By bringing Uke's arm up and away from his body, Tori is making it easier for her to slip her right arm underneath Uke's right arm and get the grip she needs.

There are variations to this grip where the same principles apply. The most common variation is when Tori changes to a left-handed traditional sleeve and lapel grip while Uke maintains a traditional right-handed sleeve and lapel grip. The important point here is that Uke is gripping Tori's left lapel with his right hand but Tori is now gripping Uke's right lapel with her left hand. This means that Tori's left arm now lies next to Uke's right arm. For this to work,

Fig. 28 Variation to Ippon Seoi Nage grip.

Fig. 27 Traditional Ippon Seoi Nage grip.

Tori's left arm must be higher than Uke's right arm, so Tori must get a higher grip on Uke's lapel than Uke can get on Tori's lapel. If Tori does get this higher grip, her left arm will lie along the top of Uke's right arm. When Tori turns in for the throw, she again clamps Uke's left arm with her right arm. To do this, she passes her right arm under the upper part of Uke's right arm and clamps the arm at the top of the tricep. Again, it is vital that Tori clamps Uke's right arm between her bicep and forearm like a vice. The inside of Tori's elbow lies against the head of Uke's tricep, and the bend of Tori's elbow allows her bicep and forearm to clamp Uke's right arm.

What makes this grip so effective is that Uke's right arm is now effectively trapped by both of Tori's arms. Tori's left arm lies on top of Uke's right arm and therefore traps the arm from above while Tori's right arm clamps under Uke's right arm and therefore traps the arm from underneath. This helps ensure that Tori keeps a good grip of Uke throughout the throw and therefore helps Tori keep control of the throw. Also, many judo players prefer this grip because they feel it is a stronger grip and therefore a more effective grip with which to break Uke's balance. With Ippon Seoi Nage, it is vital that Tori brings Uke up on to his toes and gets him to move forward. Tori's left arm, and therefore grip, plays a crucial role in pulling Uke forward and up because Tori must let go of Uke with her right hand as she turns in. At this moment, Tori must control Uke's body with her left arm. Many judo players find it easier to keep control of Uke's body if they grip Uke's lapel with their left hand rather than his sleeve.

Entry

Tori needs to bring Uke forward and up. Ideally, Uke should be on his toes with his weight coming forward. Tori will therefore usually take a step forward towards Uke and pull Uke towards her as she steps forward. From a right-hand grip, Tori steps forward with her right foot. However, Tori does not step forward in a straight line, instead Tori's first step is across Uke's body. In other words, Tori steps forward and puts her right foot down almost in line with Uke's right foot. The right side of Tori's body is now facing the front of Uke's body.

Tori then releases her right-hand grip from Uke's left lapel and turns in anticlockwise 180 degrees. Tori does this by swivelling on the ball of the right foot that she first stepped forward with. By swivelling on the ball of the right foot, Tori is able to bring the left leg around and into line with the right leg. Tori, started the throw by facing Uke, but by swivelling around 180 degrees, Tori is now facing away from Uke. Tori should be standing right in front of Uke.

It is vital in performing this throw correctly that Tori's feet are in the right position, her hips are at the right height and her grip on Uke's arm is secure. Tori's feet should be about shoulder-width apart and slightly closer together than Uke's two feet. Both Tori and Uke's feet are pointing in the same direction. It is important that Tori's feet are not too far apart because if they are, Tori will not be able to get the lift and control that she wants and needs for the throw.

It is essential that Tori's hips are lower than Uke's hips. Unless your opponent is much taller than you, this can only be achieved by bending your legs. A common mistake Tori can make is to bend forward in an attempt to get low and underneath Uke. This will ruin the contact Tori must have between her back and Uke's chest and make completion of the throw very difficult. Tori must get underneath Uke to be able to throw Uke over her shoulder and this can only be achieved by bringing Uke up on to his toes and by Tori bending her legs. If Uke is shorter than Tori, then she will have to bend her legs more. The shorter Uke is in comparison to Tori, the more Tori must bend at the knee.

Fig. 29 Ippon Seoi Nage.

Contact Point

Tori now has the top of her back against Uke's chest, and her shoulder blades should be touching Uke. Tori's feet should be approximately shoulder-width apart and facing in the same direction as Uke's feet. Tori should have a secure grip of Uke's right arm, and the back of her pelvis should be touching the front of Uke's pelvis. Tori's hips must be lower than those of Uke's. Any space between Tori and Uke will lead to trouble because it is vital that at this stage of the throw Tori keeps Uke moving forward. The close contact of Tori's back and pelvis to Uke ensures that Tori has the control she needs to throw Uke. If Uke is moving forward, Tori can throw him over her shoulder by simply straightening her legs and bending forward at the same time. What Tori has effectively done is to bring the top half of Uke's body forward by bending forward herself. However, Tori's hips and legs have blocked Uke's legs from moving forward, and Uke is now stretched out on Tori's back. By straightening her legs Tori has kept Uke moving forward because her hips have lifted Uke's feet from the ground, this allows Uke's momentum to keep moving him forward, and Uke then quite literally rolls over Tori's shoulder.

Completion

Tori has Uke stretched out on her back, she has a firm grip of Uke's right arm and has lifted Uke up so his feet are no longer on the ground: she has complete control of Uke's body. Tori needs to keep Uke rolling forward, otherwise Uke could become stuck on Tori's back. To maintain and control Uke's descent to the floor, Tori must drop her right shoulder towards the ground and turn her head to the left. To execute this movement, Tori should look down at her left foot. Tori drops her right shoulder and turns her head to the left because she does not want to slow Uke's forward momentum down. Tori has set the throw up so that Uke is forced into falling forward over her shoulder. By dropping her right shoulder towards the floor, Tori makes sure that her shoulder does not block Uke from falling forward and she creates the space she wants Uke to fall forward into.

When Uke has rolled over her back, Tori will straighten her back so that she finishes the throw standing upright, legs slightly bent, with a firm grip of Uke's right arm. By straightening up and keeping a strong grip of Uke's right sleeve, Tori will actually pull Uke into the correct position for the breakfall. The pulling action of Tori on the sleeve helps pull Uke around so that he lands on his back. This is important for several reasons, the first being that it helps protect Uke from injury. The second is that it is only by throwing your opponent with force and landing your opponent on their back that you are going to score an Ippon and win the fight in competition. It is really frustrating for Tori to execute this throw perfectly but, due to a lack of control at the end of the throw, miss the Ippon score and then, to compound the error, go on to lose the fight later on. Put your opponent away when you have the chance.

Uke

The trajectory Uke follows when he is thrown with Ippon Seoi Nage is exactly the same as when Uke practises Mae Mawari Ukemi. Judo players practise their breakfalls over and over again so that they have no fear of being thrown and therefore enjoy their judo practice whether they are Tori or Uke. If Uke has practised his Mae Mawari Ukemi, he should have little difficulty with Tori throwing him with Ippon Seoi Nage. The important principles to adhere to are that the head is tucked in and that it does not touch the mat. It is the back of Uke's shoulders that must first make contact with the mat.

O Uchi Gari (Major Inner Reap)

O Uchi Gari is a throw that when executed properly is very fast. This makes O Uchi Gari very effective because it is a throw that can often catch your opponent unawares. The speed of O Uchi Gari makes this throw very difficult to defend against because it is a throw that is difficult to anticipate. The speed of the throw comes from the fact that it is technically relatively simple. Tori simply steps in, wraps her leg around Uke's leg and uses her leg to pull Uke's leg away from underneath him. Uke can no longer use this leg to support his weight and therefore falls to the ground. For the beginner, O Uchi Gari is a simple but effective throw for the experienced judo player and it is a throw that can be used in combination with many other throws. O Uchi Gari is therefore a throw that you will see used at all levels of competition from junior club to senior international . This should make O Uchi Gari a fundamental part of every judo player's repertoire of throws.

Breaking Balance

To break Uke's balance, Tori needs to drive Uke backwards. However, it is important that Tori does not push Uke straight back because she does not want Uke to step backwards and therefore avoid the throw. Tori wants to drive Uke backwards and pin most of his weight on to his left leg, so the ideal balance breaker for O Uchi Gari is to the left back corner (see Figure 19). For Tori to break Uke's balance without Uke stepping backwards, her hands have to perform two different actions at the same time. Tori's left hand (that grips Uke's right sleeve) will pull. This will help with Uke's entry into the throw and stop Uke stepping backwards with his right leg. Tori's right hand (which grips the lapel) will drive Uke back and to the left back corner (left back corner relative to Uke). This will pin most of Uke's weight on to his left leg and stops Uke stepping back with his left leg, thus setting him up for the throw. This dual action by Tori's hands is important because it breaks Uke's balance and sets him up for the throw but also prevents Uke from being able to escape or counter O Uchi Gari with a throw of his own.

However, Tori can only use her right hand to pin Uke's weight down on to his left leg once she has got in close to Uke. This is an example of how breaking balance and the entry to the throw are all part of one movement. Judo coaches break a throw down into separate parts when they teach a technique to help students learn a complex movement. It is only when the student can put the different parts together in sequence that the student can execute this complex movement correctly and therefore execute the throw correctly. With O Uchi Gari, it is impossible completely to separate the movements required for breaking Uke's balance from the movements required for Tori to start her entry into the throw.

To do this correctly, Tori will actually first pull Uke forward with both her left and right hands. At the same time, Tori will step forward with her right leg and bring her body up close to Uke. At this moment, Tori will drive Uke back and to the left back corner with her right hand. This change from pull to push with the right hand can only be effective if Tori gets the entry into the throw correct. It is the correct entry into the throw that is the trigger for Tori to change the action of her right hand from a pull to a push. It is also essential that throughout the throw Tori maintains a strong pull on Uke's sleeve with her left hand.

Grip

The most effective grip for this throw is the classical sleeve and lapel grip as this grip is best suited to the dual pulling and pushing action of Tori's hands. A sleeve and collar grip can be used, but Tori will find it harder to use the right hand to pin Uke's weight on to his left leg. It is best to learn this throw first with a traditional sleeve and lapel grip and then progress to a sleeve and collar grip.

For O Uchi Gari to be effective, Tori must keep the majority of Uke's weight on his left leg. To do this, Tori pushes backwards and down with her right hand on Uke's left shoulder, pinning Uke's weight on to his left leg. The most effective way for Tori to achieve this from a sleeve and lapel grip is to move the right hand up and into line with Uke's collarbone. There is no need for Tori to let go of Uke's lapel because the jacket is loose and will give Tori the freedom to move her right hand higher without having to let go of the jacket. Tori will use this new position for the right hand to drive her right hand forward. However, to make sure that Uke's weight remains on his left leg, Tori will not drive the right hand straight forward but instead will drive the right hand up and over Uke's left shoulder. So while Tori's grip of Uke's lapel does not change, the position of the right hand does. Tori needs to move the right hand up and over the top of Uke's left shoulder without letting go of Uke's left lapel.

Entry

Tori pulls Uke towards her, at the same time stepping forward with her right leg. Tori places her right foot in between Uke's legs. If you looked at a clock and Uke was standing at twelve o'clock with his feet at five to and five past twelve, Tori places her right foot on twelve o'clock. Tori then brings her left foot up close to the back of her right foot. The left leg is slightly bent and the foot is pointed so that the toes and ball of the foot are in contact with the floor. The position of the left foot is the same as if Tori were trying to stand on her toes. The inside of the left ankle is in line with the Achilles tendon of the right foot, which means the toes and ball of the left foot rest on the mat just outside the line of the right side of the right foot. Tori brings the left foot up behind the right foot because she will need to drive off her left leg to produce the power needed for the throw. It is the left leg that will drive Tori forward and Uke backwards. It is Tori's right leg that will reap Uke's left leg away.

Contact Point

Tori must pay particular attention to the position of her head and body as she enters. It is important that Tori keeps good body contact with Uke because any gaps between the two of them will give Uke an opportunity to

Fig. 30 O Uchi Gari.

escape. Tori keeps her head on the right side of Uke's body, even though she is attacking Uke's left leg with her right leg. In other words, Tori must keep her head on the opposite side of Uke's body to the side that she is attacking. If Tori is attacking Uke's left side, her head must be on the right side; if Tori is attacking Uke's right side, her head must be on the left side. In this case, Tori keeps her head on the right side of Uke. The position of Tori's head is important because it does two important things. The first is that it helps Tori keep her balance and therefore control of the throw. The second is that it prevents Uke slipping Tori off to the left side of his body so that he can escape or counter the throw.

Tori slides her right leg between Uke's legs, pushing the right leg straight forward. Tori's right leg is almost straight as she pushes the right leg forward and the toes of the right foot are pointed. The left leg is pushing the right leg forward and brings the weight of Tori's entire body forward and down against Uke's chest and left shoulder. Tori then reaps her right leg to the right, trapping Uke's left leg. Put simply, the right leg of Tori wraps itself around Uke's left leg. This reaping action of Tori's right leg is similar to that of a snake wrapping itself around a pole. The temptation is for Tori to lift her right foot up from the mat as she wraps her leg around Uke's left leg but this would be a mistake. To keep Tori's weight driving forward and to keep the momentum of the throw pushing Uke backwards, Tori should keep the pointed toes of her right foot in contact with the mat. In effect, Tori draws a circle with her right foot around Uke's left foot as she wraps her right leg around Uke's left leg.

Tori's right arm never straightens out. This means that

her body is kept close to Uke and the forward momentum generated by her left leg drives Uke backwards. Uke's leg is trapped so he cannot step backwards, but Tori's upper body is driving him backwards so that the two bodies of Tori and Uke slant down towards the mat together. This gives Uke no chance to shift his weight and escape: it is by keeping her head on the right side of Uke's body that Tori keeps her weight centred so Uke cannot escape or counter.

Completion

Tori has wrapped her right leg around Uke's left leg and now has control of his left leg; because Tori is driving forward, she can keep her sweeping leg wrapped around Uke's left leg throughout the throw. If Tori remained standing upright and only hooked Uke's leg, then Uke would escape by lifting his leg over Tori's right leg and stepping backwards. If Tori loses control of Uke's left leg, she loses control of the throw. It is not until Uke lands on the mat and the throw is over that Tori releases her right leg from Uke's left leg.

There is also a twist to Tori's attack. When Tori wraps her right leg around Uke's left leg, Tori starts to reap her right leg to Uke's left. This reaping action is best described by the action of the pointed toes of her right foot drawing a circle on the mat. Tori's right leg wraps around Uke's left leg and makes a circle in a clockwise direction. This twists Tori's body around to her right and, because her body is so close to Uke's and she has control of Uke, this movement twists Uke around to his left. By twisting Uke to his left, Tori has continued to force Uke's weight on to his left

Fig. 31 Finishing position for O Uchi Gari.

leg and Uke cannot put his weight down on his left leg because Tori is sweeping this leg away.

The bodies of Tori and Uke are glued together by Tori's forward and downward drive. Tori's right hand is pushing down on Uke's left shoulder. Tori's right arm is still bent so the right arm exerts a tremendous downward force on Uke's left shoulder, forcing him backwards and down on to the mat. Tori's left arm is still locking Uke's right arm so that Uke can't slip out. Tori's right leg is reaping outward in a circle, taking Uke's left leg away from him. Tori drives Uke back and down on to the mat.

It is important that Tori does not stop driving forward until Uke lands on his back. O Uchi Gari requires a proper follow through, otherwise Uke will twist out of the throw. When demonstrating the throw, Tori will usually remain standing and lower Uke to the mat when completing the throw. This makes the practice of the throw safer and allows Tori to concentrate on perfecting the dynamics of the throw correctly. However, this will not work in competition. If Tori does not maintain the momentum of the throw by driving Uke back and down on to his back, then Uke can twist on to his side at the last minute. This means Uke will land on his side and not his back. Tori will still score for the throw but not as heavily as if she had landed Uke on his back. If Tori lands Uke on his back, it is an Ippon score and the fight is over. However, if Tori lands Uke on his side, she will probably at best score a Wazari, which will only give her seven points and means Uke gets to fight on. If Tori is practising this throw for competition purposes, she needs to practise the throw with a proper follow through, which means following Uke to the mat.

When Tori follows Uke to the mat, she must keep her body as close to Uke's as possible. The drive of her right hand forces Uke down on to his back but the pull of her left hand keeps Uke's upper body close to Tori. The combined push and pull of Tori's two hands makes it very difficult for Uke to twist or wriggle out of the throw. The reaping action of Tori's right leg that traps Uke's left leg keeps Uke's lower body close to Tori and prevents Uke from regaining his balance. The drive from Tori's left leg allows Tori to use the whole of her body weight to drive Uke backwards and on to the mat. Tori should land Uke on his back and finish on her knees in between Uke's legs (see Figure 31).

Uke

With O Uchi Gari, Uke is thrown backwards so a good Ushiro Ukemi is essential. The danger for any Uke thrown backwards is that of not tucking the head in and of throwing out the hands to break the fall. The back of the head and the wrists are not designed to hit the ground heavily and take the weight of a falling body. Usually what happens when a person falls like this is that they get concussion and/or a broken wrist. To fall backwards properly, it is essential that Uke tucks his head in so that his chin is touching his chest and that he does not put his hands out to the side to help break his fall.

Conclusion

The action for each of the throws described in this book should be one continuous movement. However, each throw is made up of a series of precise and specific movements. When you first learn how to perform a throw, the throw should be broken down into stages to make it easier to learn each of the precise movements that are involved in each stage. Only once each stage has been mastered can you put the stages together to form one sequence of movements that make up a particular throw. The throws described in this book are broken down into specific stages to help you with this process. It is important when you learn any throw that you spend the time to get each stage right. The time spent on perfecting each stage will be the foundation of good technique and getting the throw right.

The relationship between Tori and Uke is crucial to this learning process. When you first practise a throw, it is important that you have a cooperative Uke. Uke stands still and lets Tori throw him because Tori is beginning to learn the throw and needs to concentrate on perfecting the specific skills necessary for each stage of the throw. When each stage has been mastered, Tori will put each stage together to perform the whole movement smoothly. At this point, the role of Uke changes. A cooperative Uke is not realistic because your opponent will not be co-operative in competition. When you practise a throw, you must practise exactly what you need to do under pressure in the heat of competition. What you practise is what you will do under pressure. It is really important, therefore, that as Tori becomes better at a throw, her practice should develop and reflect the reality of competition as much as possible. Uke should become less helpful as it is essential that Tori develops her ability to execute the throw on the move. If at any stage Tori finds this process difficult, she should go back a step and make sure that she can execute each stage correctly before moving forward and practising the throw on the move and at speed. Good technique can only develop from careful and properly structured practice.

CHAPTER 4

GROUNDWORK (NE-WAZA)

The principle objectives to fighting on the ground are to gain control of your opponent, pin them on their back and then make them submit. A pin is a hold that quite literally pins an opponent on their back in a position where they are unable to attack. There are generally two types of submissions: those that could suffocate an opponent and those that could cause injury to one of the joints of the body. In judo, a competitor is expected to submit when they are caught with a submission technique that they cannot escape. A judo player can submit either verbally or by tapping out. Tapping out is where a player submits by tapping their opponent or the mat. Tapping out is important because a player cannot always verbally submit if their opponent is trying to suffocate them. A player can submit by tapping with their hands or their feet, this is because a player may not always be able to tap out with their hands as their opponent could have their arms tied up in a pin. A player who does not release an opponent when they submit is putting their opponent's health at risk. Such a player would be expelled from any competition or judo club because this behaviour is unacceptable and dangerous. Likewise, any player who refuses to submit risks unconsciousness or serious injury.

In competition, a fight would never start on the ground; it is only when a player has thrown their opponent to the floor that the fight can continue on the ground. If a player throws their opponent to the ground with control, force and velocity and lands their opponent squarely on their back, the player automatically wins the contest with an Ippon score. However, if a player throws their opponent to the ground and one of these essential elements (control, force, velocity, or on their back) is missing, they will score a Wazari or Yuko and the fight will continue on the ground. If neither fighter can gain an advantage on the ground, then the referee will stop the fight and stand the two fighters up. The fight will then be started again from the standing position. This is why the completion phase of any throw is so important. If a player cannot throw their opponent to the ground with an Ippon score, it is essential that they keep control of their

opponent's body after the throw has been completed so that they can establish a dominant position on the ground as quickly as possible.

Fighting on the ground is a continuation of a fight that started in the stand-up position. Any advantage gained in the stand-up position needs to be used to help gain or maintain an advantage on the floor. It is important, therefore, that a player does not simply throw their opponent to the ground and assume that they have won the fight. Instead, a good judo player will always follow their opponent to the ground and try to establish a dominant position as quickly as possible rather than wait for the referee to score an Ippon. When learning new techniques it is important to break each technique down into sections that help a new student learn new complex motor skills. As a student progresses so the sections can be put together to form one continuous movement or sequence of movements. When a student first learns a throw or a pinning technique on the floor, they will learn each technique in isolation so that they can focus on learning the specific motor skills necessary for that technique. However, as they progress, a good judo player should practise putting the throws and groundwork skills together. Each throw should lead into a hold or dominant position on the floor and the two should not always be practised in isolation. Just as breaking an opponent's balance should lead to a throw, a throw should lead to a pin, which should then lead to a lock, choke or strangle.

However, a pin does not have to lead to a submission for a player to win a fight. If a player follows their opponent to the floor and pins them on their back for 25 seconds, then they will win the fight. This applies to all judo players, whereas chokes, strangles and joint locks can only be practised by adults. In judo you are considered an adult at sixteen years of age. Submission skills are important but are only relevant to adult players. What is more, it is impossible to apply these submission techniques effectively if you have not first established the correct position from which to apply these techniques. This requires a player first to throw and pin their opponent to the ground.

It is only when a player has control of their opponent on the ground that they can effectively apply a choke, strangle or arm lock. If a player does not have the technical skills to control their opponent on the ground and pin them first, they will not have the technical skills necessary to apply any submission techniques. This book covers the core skills that a judo player needs to compete, so this book will focus on the basic pins that every judo player must learn to be able to control their opponent on the ground. The techniques discussed in this book are therefore relevant to both junior and senior players.

Fundamental to the practice of judo on the ground is the process of gaining and retaining a position of advantage or control over an opponent. This is a dynamic process where a judo player is constantly on the move, never allowing their opponent to settle or apply counter-techniques. The player's opponent is constantly trying to upset this process by developing an opportunity to escape and then gain control themselves. The pin is the culmination of this process, where a judo player has been able to gain such a dominant position over their opponent that they can no longer fight back. The successful application of a pin depends upon the position of a judo player's body in relation to that of their opponent. To escape a pin, an opponent will try to move their body and therefore alter the position of their body. A good judo player must be able to counter their opponent's efforts to escape by adjusting their body to a new and suitable position. This may simply involve small adjustments to the pin the player already has or may involve major changes such as moving to a new pin. The important principle is that a good judo player can always alter their position so that the point at which their opponent bears the weight of their body remains unchanged.

To apply a pin, a judo player uses the downward pressure of their body to prevent an opponent from moving. The application of this downward force relies upon body weight, not muscular strength. This is a fundamental principle of groundwork that is very difficult to put into practice. The temptation for a judo player in a dominant position on the ground is to try to use force to keep their opponent from moving by pushing their opponent back into the ground. This actually provides their opponent with an opportunity to escape because the player is now committed to one position and cannot readily adjust to a new one. If the opponent can disturb the player's position of control, then it is very difficult for the player to react and adjust in time to prevent a counter-attack.

It is vital that when a player practises the pins described in this book, good technique is employed. To develop good technique, the first step is to apply the pin correctly with a cooperative Uke. The second step is to maintain the pin when Uke tries to escape and the final step is to gain and maintain the pin when Uke is uncooperative. If a player has

to use strength at any stage, then that player can improve upon their technique. To be able to achieve the third stage with smooth, skilful movements that require the minimum of effort demands a very high level of practice and learning. However, if a player is going to execute good technique under the pressure of competition and a stronger opponent, then brute strength will be of limited use and good technique will be essential.

The purpose of this chapter is to introduce the reader to the pins that form the core skills that a judo player will need to compete effectively on the ground. Each pin is broken down in to the following stages:

1. **Grip** For the description of the grip I will assume that Tori is right-handed.
2. **Body** This section describes the position Tori must put her body in relative to Uke's body to execute the pin correctly. This is crucial if Tori is going to maximize the downward pressure of her body on Uke.
3. **Tip** With each pin, Tori can make small adjustments to improve her position or make it more difficult for Uke to escape. This section highlights some of these adjustments.
4. **Escapes** There is always a counter to any technique. For Uke there is always the potential to escape and this section is for Uke and the techniques he can try to apply to escape the pin.

Once again, for the purposes of this book Tori is a girl and Uke a boy. If I refer to 'she' or 'her', I am referring to Tori; if I refer to 'he' or 'him', I am referring to Uke. This should help clarify the different roles of Tori and Uke in the description for each of the following pins. Again, Tori is dressed in a blue gi and Uke in a white gi for the figures as this will help make it easier to identify them.

Hon Kesa Gatame (Scarf Hold)

The Hon part of Hon Kesa Gatame means 'true': the 'true scarf hold'. However, some judo schools do not use the Hon and simply refer to this pin as Kesa Gatame. Both terms are correct and are commonly used. Kesa Gatame is usually the first pin a new student will learn. Part of the reason for this is that in many cases Tori does not have to make too many adjustments to her grip or body position after she has thrown Uke to apply this pin effectively. So Kesa Gatame is a relatively simple pin to learn early on and one that naturally leads on from fighting in the stand-up position. However, Kesa Gatame is also a very effective pin and is common in many other grappling martial arts such as Brazilian ju-jitsu and wrestling.

Grip

Tori places her right arm around Uke's neck so that the crook of her elbow is behind the base of his neck; Tori's arm is therefore wrapped around the back of Uke's neck like a scarf. As well as being referred to as a scarf hold, this right-arm grip can also be referred to as the lapel around the neck.

Tori has a left-hand grip of Uke's right sleeve. The sleeve grip is identical to the one used in the standing position for a traditional sleeve and lapel grip. This is important because if Tori throws Uke with a traditional sleeve and lapel grip, it is the right arm and not the left that Tori must adjust to gain Kesa Gatame. Tori takes control of Uke's right arm by pulling it in tight against her body. This should bring Uke's right hand up underneath Tori's left armpit. If Tori does adjust her left hand, it will be to bring the left hand higher up the right sleeve of Uke. This will give Tori greater control of Uke's right arm and make an escape for Uke more difficult. Tori grips the back of Uke's sleeve over the head of Uke's tricep.

Body

Tori sits on her bottom next to Uke. Her legs are at right angles to Uke's body and her right hip is next to Uke's ribs. It is important that Tori's bottom is in contact with the ground as this is vital if Tori is going to maintain a dominant position. If Tori's bottom is not in contact with the ground, then Uke can wriggle his body underneath Tori and move Tori's body out of position. Tori has her legs spread to maximize the stability of her position; in judo, this is called a 'good base'. If Uke struggles, then Tori needs to be able to move her legs and thereby adjust her balance or base so that she can maintain a strong downward pressure on Uke's body. Tori must relax and let her body weight drive down upon the centre of Uke's chest, and a slight twisting action by Tori's body will help. This twisting action of the body is helped by Tori maintaining a strong pull with her left hand on Uke's right sleeve and a strong hugging action by her right arm on Uke's neck. This twisting action will increase the downward pressure exerted by Tori on Uke's chest and ribs, making it more difficult for Uke to escape, and will give Tori better control of Uke's body. This downward pressure will also make it more difficult for Uke to breathe. Any difficulty Uke has with his breathing will lead to fatigue and weaken any attempts he may make to counter-attack or escape.

Tip

If Tori can keep Uke's head off the ground, she will make it much more difficult for Uke to escape. Uke needs contact between both the back of his head and shoulders and the

Fig. 32 Hon Kesa Gatame.

Fig. 33 Hon Makura Kesa Gatame.

ground to give him the balance and drive that he will need to move Tori's body and escape. By bringing her wrist and forearm in tight against the back of Uke's neck, Tori can prevent Uke pushing his head back against the mat. A variation to Kesa Gatame that works on this principle is Makura Kesa Gatame (pillow scarf hold). With Makura Kesa Gatame, Tori pushes her right hand through so that her right hand can grip the inside of her trousers on her right leg. The purpose of Makura Kesa Gatame is to strengthen the hold Tori has around Uke's neck and make it much more difficult for Uke to push his head and shoulders back against the ground.

Escapes

The bridge and roll technique can be used to escape most pins, not just Kesa Gatame. It is a technique that any good ground fighter must be able to execute under pressure and it is a technique that can be used in a variety of different situations. The bridge and roll technique will form the basis of the escape for each of the pins described in this book. For each escape, there will be small variations to the technique depending upon the pin that Tori is

applying. However, the fundamental principles that form the bridge and roll technique will remain the same.

The bridge component to this technique is similar to a bridge in gymnastics. Uke lies flat on his back with his legs bent so that his feet are flat against the floor. To bridge, Uke pushes with his feet so that his legs start to straighten and his hips drive up towards the ceiling. His back is arched so that the only parts of his body in contact with the mat are his feet and the back of his shoulders and head. The difference between the bridge in gymnastics and in judo is that in judo Uke does not use his hands to raise his shoulders from the mat. In judo, it is important that the back of the shoulders are pressed firmly back against the mat and that Uke's arms are free and that he is able to grip Tori.

The roll brings in a twisting motion to the bridge. This means that Uke does not simply bridge straight up but instead bridges up and to one side. When Uke bridges, he pushes with both his feet so that his legs start to straighten and his hips are driven up towards the ceiling. However, as Uke pushes with both feet, he also twists his hips. This means that when Uke is in the bridge position, one hip is higher than the other, one shoulder is raised off the ground and the other shoulder is pushed back firmly against the floor. So when Uke has his back arched, the only parts of his body that are in contact with the mat are his feet, the back of one shoulder and the back of his head. If Uke was to bridge and roll to his right, then as he pushes with his feet, he also twists his hips to the right so that his left hip is higher than his right hip, his left shoulder is raised from the mat and the back of his right shoulder is pressed firmly back against the mat. If Uke was to bridge and roll to his left, then he would twist his hips to the left so that his right hip is higher than his left hip, his right shoulder is raised from the mat and the back of his left shoulder is pressed firmly back against the mat. In Figure 34, Uke is executing the bridge and roll to his left.

To use the bridge and roll technique to escape Kesa Gatame, Uke must get his body as close to Tori as possible. In Figure 32, Tori is at right angles to Uke and all of her weight is pressing down on the centre of his chest. To escape, Uke must stop Tori pushing down on the centre of his chest. This is very difficult to achieve if Tori keeps her body at right angles to Uke, so Uke must change his body position in relation to Tori. His goal is to get his body as close to Tori as possible. To achieve this, Uke rotates his body in a clockwise direction; the perfect position is if Uke can get his right hip to touch Tori's back. The closer Uke can get to Tori, the more effective Uke's bridging action will be in executing the escape.

When Uke has got as close as possible to Tori, he bridges. This bridging action drives Tori forward. Tori still has the pin but Uke's bridging action has relieved the pressure on the centre of his chest by driving Tori forward. By relieving the pressure on the centre of his chest, Uke can now roll. To roll, Uke twists both his shoulders and hips to the left. This twist brings Uke's right hip up higher than his left, it also brings his right shoulder up off the floor, while his left shoulder stays pressed down against the mat. In effect, Uke has raised the right side of his body from the floor. When Uke raises the right side of his body from the mat he brings Tori with him. This works because Uke has hooked Tori with his right arm. In Figure 35, Uke is

Fig. 34 Bridge and roll to the left.

Fig. 35 Uke escapes Kesa Gatame with a bridge and roll.

using his right arm to catch Tori but his whole body brings Tori across his body.

To put Uke in Kesa Gatame, Tori put her right arm around Uke's neck and keeps a strong left-hand grip of Uke's right sleeve. Tori took control of Uke's right arm by pulling it in tight against her body. This brought Uke's right hand up tight underneath Tori's left armpit. By extending his right arm, Uke hooks Tori with his right forearm underneath

Fig. 36 Kuzure Kesa Gatame.

her armpit. Uke can strengthen this hook by extending his left arm and holding his right wrist with his left hand. This hook effectively locks Tori against Uke so when Uke twists his body, his arms draw Tori across his body.

As Uke draws Tori across his body, he continues to twist his body so he lands Tori on her back. Uke can now sit up next to Tori in the same position that Tori was in when she pinned Uke in Kesa Gatame. Uke has now pinned Tori in Kuzure Kesa Gatame (broken scarf hold). The difference between Kuzure Kesa Gatame and Kesa Gatame is in the position of the right arm. With Kesa Gatame, Tori's right arm was around the back of Uke's neck; with Kuzure Kesa Gatame, Uke's right arm is underneath the left armpit of Tori. Uke has not only escaped from Tori's pin (Kesa Gatame), but has now put Tori in a pin of his own (Kuzure Kesa Gatame). His finishing position is identical to the position Tori was in originally except that his right arm is still underneath Tori's armpit rather than around her neck.

Hons Mune Gatame (Chest Hold)

The correct application of Mune Gatame depends upon the ability of Tori to control Uke with downward pressure on the centre of his chest. For Uke to escape any pin, he needs to turn his body or sit up so that his back is no longer in contact with the mat. If Tori's weight is pushing down through the centre of Uke's chest, then Uke will find it very difficult to move at all, making an escape very difficult. What is more, this constant downward pressure on the centre of the chest makes it very difficult for Uke to breathe, which means he can fatigue very quickly. This constant downward pressure on an opponent's chest is a fundamental part of gaining and then maintaining a dominant position in ground fighting. A good drill for Tori is to take each of the pins described in this book and keep moving from one pin to the other without any change in the downward pressure she applies to the centre of Uke's chest. Mune Gatame is a useful pin to learn because of the emphasis placed upon the application of this downward pressure upon the centre of Uke's chest. The correct application of Mune Gatame helps Tori develop the balance and understanding necessary to gaining and maintaining dominant positions through downward pressure on an opponent's chest.

Grip

Tori places her left arm around the back of Uke's neck so that the crook of her elbow is behind the base of Uke's neck. Tori reaches her right arm around and underneath Uke's left armpit so that her forearm lies flat against the floor and underneath Uke's left shoulder. Tori's right forearm is parallel with Uke's body and her right hand almost next to Uke's left ear. Unless Uke is much bigger than Tori, Tori should then be able to clasp her hands together, making the grip stronger and giving her better control of Uke. When Tori clasps her hands together, it is important that she does not interlink her fingers as any pressure applied by Uke on Tori's hands could trap her hands together. This could restrict Tori's ability to change position and could trap her in a countermove.

Tori's grip should allow her to apply a strong clamping action on Uke with her arms. It is important to note that it is Tori's arms that provide the grip and not her hands. Her arms are around the back of Uke's neck and left shoulder, and by squeezing her arms together Tori pulls her chest in tight against Uke's chest.

Body

The centre of Tori's chest lies directly above the centre of Uke's chest. Tori's chin lies just above the top of Uke's left shoulder. Tori's left shoulder lies next to the right side of Uke's neck and jaw. Tori's body lies at right angles to Uke's body so that their bodies together form the shape of the letter 'T'. Tori's left hip is in line with Uke's shoulders. The front of the left hip should be pressed down firmly against the mat. Any gap between the front of the left hip and the mat gives Uke an opportunity to escape. By dropping the front of the hip down against the mat, Tori makes the escape more difficult for Uke and increases the downward pressure on Uke's chest. Tori can vary the position of her left leg by bending the leg and bringing the left knee in tight against the side of Uke's head. Again, the important point here is not to provide Uke with any gaps that he can use to escape. The left leg must either be bent and the left knee pressed tightly against the side of Uke's head or the left leg must be straight and the front of the left hip pushed firmly down into the ground.

The higher Tori's hips are from the ground, the easier it is for Uke to wriggle his body underneath Tori and move her out of position. Tori needs to drive her hips down and maximize the downward pressure she applies to Uke's body. It is important that Tori spreads her legs so that she can use her hips to counter any attempt Uke might make to escape. By spreading her legs, Tori can maximize the stability of her position and her base. Tori must relax to let her body weight drive down upon the centre of Uke's chest and the clamping action of Tori's grip will help.

Tori bends her right leg so that her right knee is pressed firmly against Uke's right hip. The inside of Tori's right knee should lie against the floor and the top of the knee is driven into the side of Uke's hip. Tori uses her right knee to control Uke's hips. If Uke can turn his hips he can move his body and threaten Tori's dominant position. So by

Fig. 37 Hon Mune Gatame.

driving the right knee up against his hip, Tori is limiting Uke's ability to move and therefore escape.

Tip

The most common escape from Mune Gatame is for Uke to bridge and roll. To execute this escape successfully, Uke needs to get good contact between the mat, the back of his head and his shoulders. This contact with the ground is important because it will give him the strength and drive that he needs to move Tori's body and escape. The more control Tori has of Uke's head and shoulders, the more difficult it is for Uke to escape. Tori can increase the control she has of Uke's head and shoulders by using the clamping

Fig. 38 Kuzure Mune Gatame.

action of her grip to drive her left shoulder down firmly against Uke's neck and jaw. By driving her left shoulder tight into Uke's neck and jaw, it becomes very difficult for Uke to move his head or shoulders and therefore very difficult to escape.

A variation to Mune Gatame is Kuzure Mune Gatame (broken chest hold). The essential difference between the two pins is the position of Tori's left arm. For Mune Gatame, Tori's left arm is behind Uke's neck, while for Kuzure Mune Gatame Tori's left arm is around the top of Uke's left shoulder. With Kuzure Mune Gatame, Tori has far less control over Uke's head because her left arm circles his left shoulder rather than his head. This makes Kuzure Mune Gatame more vulnerable to a counter-attack from Uke.

Escapes

To escape Mune Gatame, Uke must stop Tori pressing all of her weight down on the centre of his chest. With a bridge and roll escape, Uke uses the bridging action to this technique to drive Tori forward. Tori still has the pin but Uke's bridging action has relieved the pressure on the centre of his chest by driving Tori forward. By relieving the pressure on the centre of his chest, Uke can now roll. To roll, Uke twists both his shoulders and hips to the left. This twist brings Uke's right hip and shoulder up off the floor, while his left shoulder stays pressed down against the mat. In effect, Uke has raised the right side of his body from the floor. When Uke raises the right side of his body from the mat he brings Tori with him.

Uke grips Tori with exactly the same grip that Tori is using to grip Uke. Uke places his left arm around the back of Tori's neck and his right arm underneath Tori's left armpit. Uke's right hand should be able to touch the back of Tori's left shoulder. Unless Tori is much bigger than Uke, Uke should then be able to clasp his hands together. Again, it is very important that when Uke clasps his hands together that he does not interlink his fingers. The strong grip Uke now has on Tori allows Uke to draw Tori across his body as he rolls out of the pin. As Uke draws Tori across his body, he continues to twist his body so that he lands Tori on her back.

Uke now adjusts his body so that it is at right angles to Tori; the best position for Uke is if Tori and Uke's bodies form the letter 'T'. There is no need for Uke to adjust his grip. Uke has used the bridge and roll technique to escape from Tori's pin (Mune Gatame) and put Tori in exactly the same pin. If Uke now takes his right arm and puts it around Tori's left leg, Uke has changed the pin from Mune Gatame to Yoko Shiho Gatame (side four quarters) (see Figure 39).

Yoko Shiho Gatame (Side Four Quarters Hold)

An advantage to Yoko Shiho Gatame is the control that it gives Tori over Uke's hips. With Mune Gatame, Tori prevents Uke from turning his hips by pressing her right knee up tight against the side of Uke's hips. With Yoko Shiho Gatame, Tori can use both her right knee and right arm to prevent Uke from turning his hips. To escape, Uke needs to use his hips, so the additional level of control that Tori has over Uke's hips with this pin makes it more difficult for Uke to use his hips to escape. However, to gain better control of Uke's hips with Yoko Shiho Gatame, Tori sacrifices some of the control she had with Mune Gatame over Uke's head and shoulders. With Mune Gatame, Tori could keep the centre of her chest directly over the centre of Uke's chest. This body position, coupled with the clamping action of her grip, allowed Tori to exert more downward pressure on Uke's chest, giving her better control of Uke's head and shoulders. The two pins are technically very similar but there are subtle differences between the two. Which pin is more appropriate depends upon the situation and factors such as the size and technical ability of an opponent. Tori may find that she needs to change from one pin to the other to increase or maintain her control of Uke.

Grip

Tori places her left arm around the back of Uke's neck so that the crook of her elbow is behind the base of his neck. Her left hand grips the top of Uke's left shoulder. Tori reaches her right arm around and underneath Uke's left leg so that the crook of her elbow lies against the back of Uke's thigh. Her right arm is wrapped around Uke's left leg so that her right hand can grip Uke's belt. If Uke is taller than Tori, Tori may not be able to reach Uke's belt; in this case, Tori can grip Uke's gi instead.

Body

The centre of Tori's chest lies above the bottom of Uke's chest or the top of his stomach. The exact position will depend on how tall Uke is in relation to Tori. The taller Uke is, the lower Tori will tend to be on Uke's body. Tori's body lies at right angles to Uke's body so that their bodies together form the shape of the letter 'T'. Tori's left hip is in line with the top of Uke's chest. The front of the left hip should be pressed down firmly against the mat. Any gap between the front of the left hip and the mat gives Uke an opportunity to escape. By dropping the front of the hip down against the mat, Tori makes the escape more difficult for Uke and increases the downward pressure on him. Tori

Fig. 39 Hon Yoko Shiho Gatame.

can vary the position of her left leg by bending the leg and bringing the left knee in tight against the side of Uke's head. Again, the important point here is not to provide Uke with any gaps that he can use to escape. The left leg must either be bent and the left knee pressed tightly against the side of Uke's head or the left leg must be straight and the front of the left hip pushed firmly down into the ground.

The higher Tori's hips are from the ground, the easier it is for Uke to wriggle his body underneath Tori and move her out of position. Tori needs to drive her hips down and maximize the downward pressure she applies to Uke's body. It is important that Tori spreads her legs so that she can use her hips to counter any attempt Uke might make to escape. By spreading her legs, Tori can maximize the stability of her position and her base. Tori must relax to let her body weight drive down upon Uke.

Tori has a choice with what she does with her right leg. The first option is to do exactly what she did with Mune Gatame. Tori bends her right leg so that her right knee is pressed firmly against Uke's right hip. The inside of Tori's right knee should lie against the floor and the top of the knee is driven into the side of Uke's hip. Tori uses her right knee to control Uke's hips and prevent him from turning. The second option is to have the right leg straight. If this is the case, the front of the right hip should be pressed down firmly against the mat. Any gap between the front of the right hip and the mat gives Uke an opportunity to escape. By dropping the front of the hip down against the

mat, Tori makes the escape more difficult for Uke and increases the downward pressure on him. If Tori has the right leg bent, then she has better control of Uke's hips; if she has her right leg straight, she increases the downward pressure on Uke. Tori can vary the position of her right leg as she wishes. This is helpful because it allows her to adjust her position and counter any attempt Uke makes to escape. To increases her control of Uke's hips, she bends her right leg; to increase her downward pressure on Uke, she straightens her right leg. The important point here is not to provide Uke with any gaps that he can use to escape. The right leg must either be bent and the right knee pressed tightly against the side of Uke's hips or the right leg must be straight and the front of the right hip pushed firmly down into the ground.

Tip

To get a good strong grip with her right arm around Uke's left leg, Tori can often make the mistake of having a relatively weak grip with her left arm around Uke's neck. This is particularly common if Uke is taller than Tori, when it can be very difficult for Tori to apply Yoko Shiho Gatame without shifting her body to her right and therefore down Uke's body. If she does this, Tori's chest is now no longer pushing down on Uke's chest. Instead, Tori's weight is pushing down on Uke's stomach. This weakens the pin because Tori has less control over Uke's head and shoulders. This makes Tori vulnerable to a counter-attack from

Fig. 40 Variation to Hon Yoko Shiho Gatame.

Uke because he can now use his head and shoulders for a bridge and roll escape. To avoid this problem, Tori can alter her right arm grip to allow for Tori being taller. Instead, Tori can grip Uke's trousers just above his left hip with her right hand. This gives the improved control of Uke's hips that Tori wants with Yoko Shiho Gatame but it also allows her to keep a strong grip with her left arm around the back of Uke's neck and therefore maintain control of Uke's head and shoulders.

A variation to Yoko Shiho Gatame is Kuzure Yoko Shiho Gatame (broken side four quarters hold). Just as with Mune Gatame and Kuzure Mune Gatame, the essential difference between the two pins is the position of Tori's left arm. For Yoko Shiho Gatame, Tori's left arm is behind

Fig. 41 Kuzure Yoko Shiho Gatame.

Uke's neck, while for Kuzure Yoko Shiho Gatame Tori's left arm is around the top of Uke's left shoulder. Again, with Kuzure Yoko Shiho Gatame, Tori has far less control over Uke's head because Tori's left arm circles his left shoulder rather than his head. This makes Kuzure Yoko Shiho Gatame much more vulnerable to a counter-attack.

Escapes

With Yoko Shiho Gatame, the bridge is more difficult for Uke because of the control Tori has over his hips. To use the bridge and roll technique to escape, Uke first needs to change the position of his body and put himself in a better position from which to attack. Uke does this by turning his body to the right, in towards Tori. If he can, Uke wants to turn his body far enough that he is almost on his right side. Uke can help this process by reaching over Tori's left shoulder and down her back with his left arm and grabbing hold of the back of her belt. As he does this, he also slides his right arm underneath the front of Tori's left hip. Uke wraps his right arm around Tori's left leg from the inside and pulls Tori's left knee in to his body. If Tori can keep her leg straight and the front of her left hip flat against the floor, Uke will find it very difficult to use this escape. However, if Tori gives Uke the slightest gap to slide his right arm through so that he can gain control of her left leg, then Tori is vulnerable to the counter-attack.

When Uke turns his body in towards Tori, Uke pulls with his left arm on the back of Tori's belt to help turn his shoulders and he pushes with his left leg to help turn his hips so that the whole of his body turns towards Tori. If Uke can turn the whole of his body in towards Tori, he will upset Tori's position by pushing Tori's chest upwards. This weakens the control Tori has over Uke's body because she can no longer apply the same downward pressure on Uke. Uke is no longer pressed firmly back down on his back, and by turning his body to the right he is now in a position to move Tori completely out of position.

The difference from previous escapes is that Uke is still not in a position to execute the bridge because he is lying on his right side and Tori still has a strong grip of his left leg. So Uke must first roll before bridging if he is to escape. Uke does this by turning the whole of his body to his left, thus drawing Tori across his body so that her head almost touches the mat on the other side of his body, the left side. At this point, Tori's body still lies at 90 degrees to Uke's body but Uke has drawn Tori's body right over the top of him so that her chest, stomach and hips are directly above him. However, her body now exerts very little downward pressure on Uke because her head is low (almost on the mat) and her hips are high, so the downward pressure of her weight is directed down towards the mat on the left side of Uke. Uke's problem is that if he continues simply to turn his body to the left, then he will simply drive Tori's head into the mat and she will be stuck on top of him. It is at this point that the bridge and Uke's right arm play a vital role.

Fig. 42 Uke turns in for the escape from Yoko Shiho Gatame.

Fig. 43 Uke draws Tori across his body as he escapes Yoko Shiho Gatame.

Uke bridges, pushing his right hip up as high as he can. This helps generate the power that Uke needs to continue to drive Tori's body up and across his body. At the same time, Uke extends his right arm up above his head and across his body (while keeping a hold of Tori's left leg). This extension of the right arm is vital because it rotates Tori's body around so that her legs can pass over Uke's head. By bringing her legs up and around his head, Uke can now draw Tori completely over his body without Tori's head blocking the escape. Uke can control Tori's legs because his right arm is wrapped around Tori's left leg, and by extending his right arm, Uke can pull Tori's legs up towards his head so that her body now lies almost parallel with his.

The bridge Uke has executed drives Tori across his body so that she lands on her back next to him. However, the power of the bridge also allows Uke to come over and across Tori's body so that he now lies in the perfect position for Kuzure Yoko Shiho Gatame. Uke does not have to adjust his grip because his right arm is already wrapped around Tori's left leg and his left arm is around the top of Tori's left shoulder. However, if Uke moves his left arm so that it is now wrapped around the back of Tori's neck, then Uke has moved from Kuzure Yoko Shiho Gatame to Yoko Shiho Gatame.

Conclusion

Fighting on the ground is a process of gaining and retaining a position of advantage or control over your opponent. Even when a judo player has been able to gain such a dominant position over their opponent that the opponent can no longer fight back, it may still be necessary for the player to adjust the position of their body to maintain their dominant position. Crucial to this whole process is the downward pressure that a judo player can exert on their opponent. A good fighter on the ground has the ability constantly to change their position so the point at which their opponent bears the weight of their body remains unchanged. The application of this downward force relies upon body weight and the correct positioning of the body in relation to the opponent, rather than muscular strength. It is the application of this constant downward pressure on the opponent's body that is fundamental to gaining and then maintaining a dominant position in ground fighting.

It is important, therefore, that when a player practises the pins described in this book, they do so with good technique and not with brute strength. The pins described in this book are not simply positions to fight for and then hold, but positions a good student should be able to move in and out of with confidence. As I mentioned earlier, an excellent drill for any judo player is to take each of the pins described in this book and keep moving from one pin to the other without any change in the downward pressure they apply to their training partner's chest.

With the techniques described in this book, the first step is to apply the pins correctly with a cooperative Uke, the second step is to maintain the pin when Uke tries to escape and the final step is to gain and maintain the pin when Uke is uncooperative. If a player has to rely on brute strength at any stage, then that player can improve upon their technique. As a studen–t progresses and their skill level improves, so the practice sessions should become more difficult. Fighting on the ground can be an exhausting process so it is important that a player can maintain a high level of performance when they are tired. Thus these techniques should be practised when a student is physically tired. In this case, the techniques should be practised at the end of a training session or when the student has been pre-fatigued with fitness drills. If a judo player is going to execute good technique under the physical and mental pressure of competition, their practice should replicate the challenges they will face. It is during practice that a student will develop the technical skills needed to control an opponent on the floor. It is vital, therefore, that each training session is structured to match the ability level of the student so that each session challenges the student and helps them progress.

It is also important to remember that any fight on the ground is a continuation of a fight that started in the stand-up position. Any advantage gained in the stand-up position needs to be used to help gain or maintain an advantage on the floor. A good judo player will always follow their opponent to the ground and try to establish a dominant position as quickly as possible. When a student first learns a technique on the floor, it is important to learn the technique in isolation so that they can focus on learning the specific motor skills necessary for that technique. However, as a student progresses, so they should practise putting the throws and groundwork skills together. Each throw should lead into a hold or dominant position on the floor and the two should not always be practised in isolation.

CHAPTER 5

PUTTING IT ALL TOGETHER

Technically, Judo is a complex sport. Any judo contest is defined by two fighters trying to execute a series of moves that flow from one technique to another. This book has isolated many of the techniques that a judo player will try and execute in a contest. To learn judo, you must isolate the techniques that define this art so that the specific skills necessary to execute each technique can be assimilated and learnt. However, it is the ability to put these individual techniques together that distinguishes the accomplished fighter.

To begin with, each technique is learnt in isolation and each technique is broken down into stages to make it easier to learn each of the precise movements that define the technique. When each stage has been mastered, a student can then put the stages together to apply the technique being learnt. All the techniques described in this book are broken down into the specific stages needed to help you with this process. It is important when you learn any technique that you spend the time necessary to get each stage right. The time spent on perfecting each stage will be the foundation of good technique and getting each technique right under pressure.

The relationship between Tori and Uke is crucial to this learning process. When you first practise a technique, it is important that you have a cooperative Uke. Uke lets Tori apply the technique because Tori needs to concentrate on perfecting the specific skills necessary for each stage of the technique. When each stage has been mastered, Tori will put each stage together to perform the whole technique smoothly. At this point, the role of Uke changes. When you practise a technique, you must practise exactly what you need to do under pressure. It is really important that as you become better at a technique, your practice should develop and reflect the reality of competition as much as possible. It is, therefore, essential that you develop the ability to execute on the move each of the throws described in this book. So, as you improve, your practice should be done on the move.

It is important with any practice that the level of difficulty matches the level of ability of the student. If the practice is too easy, nothing will be learnt because the practice session does not challenge the student and teach new skills. If the practice session is too difficult, nothing will be learnt because the student does not have the basic technical skills to be able to apply the techniques that they are trying to learn. Good technique is developed from well-structured practice sessions that are relevant to the ability and level of skill that the student possesses. This structured progression is where a good coach can really help.

If you are learning a specific throw, you should first learn the throw with an Uke who is cooperative and static. Once this has been achieved, you should still learn the throw with a cooperative Uke but on the move. Only when the throw can be executed smoothly on the move should you progress to the next level of practice. At this level, it is important for Tori to combine each throw with a hold on the ground. The primary purpose of a throw is to get an opponent on the floor on their back, while the primary purpose of a hold is to keep the opponent on their back by pinning them to the floor. Each throw should lead straight into a hold on the floor. If Tori loses control of Uke after the throw, then Uke can escape and the fight continues. However, if Tori keeps control of Uke after the throw and moves straight into a hold on the floor, Tori can win the fight by pinning Uke to the floor for 30 seconds. This is important because Tori may not always score an Ippon by throwing Uke on to his or her back in a contest. Tori cannot wait for the referee to decide if a throw was an Ippon score or not. Tori must take advantage of the throw immediately and use it as an opportunity to pin Uke to the floor with a hold. The transition from throwing an opponent to a hold on the floor is a fundamental part of judo. For this to work smoothly and effectively, Tori must practise moving from the throw straight into a hold on the floor.

In this chapter, Ray Stevens (dressed in the blue gi) takes the techniques we have focused on in this book and puts them together into a sequence of movements. In each sequence, Ray will first break his Uke's balance and then throw him. From the throw, Ray will then move straight into a hold on the floor. So instead of isolating each technique, these pictures of Ray show how techniques can be put together to form an attack. This is where your practice should lead you. First assimilate and learn the individual techniques described in this book in isolation but then put them together. Here Ray brings the throwing skills and the groundwork skills discussed in this book together.

What these pictures cannot convey is the speed at which Ray executes each technique and the speed with which Ray moves from the throw into the hold on the floor. This speed does not come from strength or power but from an ability to execute these techniques correctly, because speed comes from smooth and technically correct movements. Your movements should be slow and precise when you first learn a sequence of movements because you are learning a new skill. When you can execute the movements slowly and correctly, you can then develop the skill to execute the movements quickly and correctly. It is vital, therefore, that you first gain the ability to perform each technique correctly because the correct execution of each technique is the platform or the gateway to the next technique. What Ray demonstrates in these photographs is how the whole chain of specific movements can come together to form one complete attack.

There are seven sequences of movements photographed and each sequence contains only the techniques that have been discussed and illustrated in this book. Each of these sequences of movements form one flowing attack that starts with a throw and finishes with a hold on the floor. Each of the seven sequences that Ray performs has been photographed from his front and from his back in order to give the reader a more complete picture of how these techniques are executed. By photographing these techniques from the front and back, it is possible to illustrate much more clearly the precise detail of each technique. If you find any of the techniques difficult to execute, go back a step and practise the specific technique in isolation until you feel comfortable with the technique. Then bring the technique back into a sequence of movements that make up one specific attack. Each attack should start with a throw and finish with a hold. This is a process that you should constantly work with and refine in your practice, whatever your level of ability. The transition from standing to pinning Uke to the floor must be smooth and quick so Uke has very little opportunity to escape.

It is important to remember that Ray is dressed in the blue gi and that Uke is dressed in the white gi. References to the front and back are to Ray's front or back. So photographs taken from the front are taken from Ray's front and photographs taken from the back are taken from Ray's back.

Sequence One

Figures 44 to 73 show Ray throwing Uke with O Soto Gari and pinning Uke to the floor with Hon Kesa Gatame. Figures 44 to 54 show Ray throwing Uke with O Soto Gari from the front. Figures 55 to 59 show Ray moving from O Soto Gari into Hon Kesa Gatame from the front. Figures 60 and 61 show Ray pinning Uke with Hon Kesa Gatame from the front.

Fig. 44 O Soto Gari from the front.

Fig. 45

Fig. 46

Fig. 47

Fig. 48

Fig. 49

Fig. 51

Fig. 50

Fig. 52

Fig. 53

Fig. 55 Transition from O Soto Gari to Hon Kesa Gatame from the front.

Fig. 54

Fig. 56

Fig. 57

Fig. 60 Hon Kesa Gatame from the front.

Fig. 58

Fig. 61

Fig. 59

Figures 62 to 70 show Ray throwing Uke with O Soto Gari from the back. Figures 71 and 72 show Ray moving from O Soto Gari into Hon Kesa Gatame from the back. Figure 73 shows Ray pinning Uke with Hon Kesa Gatame from the back.

Fig. 62 O Soto Gari from the back.

Fig. 64

Fig. 63

Fig. 65

Fig. 66

Fig. 67

Fig. 68

Fig. 69

Fig. 70

Fig. 72

Fig. 71 Transition from O Soto Gari to Hon Kesa Gatame from the back.

Fig. 73 Hon Kesa Gatame from the back.

Sequence Two

Figures 74 to 101 show Ray throwing Uke with Tai Otoshi and pinning Uke to the floor with Makura Kesa Gatame. Figures 74 to 82 show Ray throwing Uke with Tai Otoshi from the front. Figures 83 and 84 show Ray moving from Tai Otoshi into Makura Kesa Gatame from the front. Figure 85 shows Ray pinning Uke with Makura Kesa Gatame from the back.

Fig. 74 Tai Otoshi from the front.

Fig. 76

Fig. 77

Fig. 75

Fig. 78

Fig. 80

Fig. 79

Fig. 81

Fig. 82

Fig. 84

Fig. 83 Transition from Tai Otoshi to Makura Kesa Gatame from the front.

Fig. 85 Makura Kesa Gatame from the back.

Figures 86 to 95 show Ray throwing Uke with Tai Otoshi from the back. Figures 96 to 98 show Ray moving from Tai Otoshi into Makura Kesa Gatame from the back. Figures 99 to 101 show Ray pinning Uke with Makura Kesa Gatame from the front.

Fig. 86 Tai Otoshi from the back.

Fig. 88

Fig. 87

Fig. 89

Fig. 90

Fig. 92

Fig. 91

Fig. 93

Fig. 94

Fig. 96 Transition from Tai Otoshi to Makura Kesa Gatame from the back.

Fig. 95

Fig. 97

Fig. 98

Fig. 100

Fig. 101

Fig. 99 Makura Kesa Gatame from the front.

Fig. 102 O Goshi from the front.

Fig. 104

Fig. 103

Sequence Three

Figures 102 to 129 show Ray throwing Uke with O Goshi and pinning Uke to the floor with Kuzure Kesa Gatame. Figures 102 to 111 show Ray throwing Uke with O Goshi from the front. Figures 112 and 113 show Ray moving from O Goshi into Kuzure Kesa Gatame from the front. Figure 114 shows Ray pinning Uke with Kuzure Kesa Gatame from the back.

Fig. 105

Fig. 106

Fig. 108

Fig. 107

Fig. 109

Fig. 110

Fig. 112 Transition from O Goshi to Kuzure Kesa Gatame from the front.

Fig. 111

Fig. 113

Fig. 114 Kuzure Kesa Gatame from the back.

Figures 115 to 126 show Ray throwing Uke with O Goshi from the back. Figures 127 and 128 show Ray moving from O Goshi into Kuzure Kesa Gatame from the back. Figure 129 shows Ray pinning Uke with Kuzure Kesa Gatame from the front.

Fig. 116

Fig. 115 O Goshi from the back.

Fig. 117

Fig. 118

Fig. 120

Fig. 119

Fig. 121

Fig. 122

Fig. 124

Fig. 123

Fig. 125

Fig. 126

Fig. 128

Fig. 127 Transition from O Goshi to Kuzure Kesa Gatame from the back.

Fig. 129 Kuzure Kesa Gatame from the front.

Sequence Four

Figures 130 to 156 show Ray throwing Uke with Uki Goshi and pinning Uke to the floor with Hon Yoko Shiho Gatame. Figures 130 to 139 show Ray throwing Uke with Uki Goshi from the front. Figures 140 and 141 show Ray moving from Uki Goshi into Hon Yoko Shiho Gatame from the front. Figure 142 shows Ray pinning Uke with Hon Yoko Shiho Gatame from the front.

Fig. 131

Fig. 132

Fig. 130 Uki Goshi from the front.

Fig. 133

Fig. 135

Fig. 134

Fig. 136

Fig. 137

Fig. 139

Fig. 138

Fig. 140 Transition from Uki Goshi to Hon Yoko Shiho Gatame from the front.

Fig. 141

Fig. 143 Uki Goshi from the back.

Fig. 142 Hon Yoko Shiho Gatame from the front.

Figures 143 to 152 show Ray throwing Uke with Uki Goshi from the back. Figures 153 to 155 show Ray moving from Uki Goshi into Hon Yoko Shiho Gatame from the back. Figure 156 shows Ray pinning Uke with Hon Yoko Shiho Gatame from the back.

Fig. 144

Fig. 145

Fig. 146

Fig. 147

Fig. 148

Fig. 149

Fig. 150

Fig. 151

Fig. 152

Fig. 153 Transition from Uki Goshi to Hon Yoko Shiho Gatame from the back.

Fig. 155

Fig. 154

Fig. 156 Hon Yoko Shiho Gatame from the back.

Fig. 157 Harai Goshi from the front.

Fig. 159

Fig. 160

Fig. 158

Sequence Five

Figures 157 to 186 show Ray throwing Uke with Harai Goshi and pinning Uke to the floor with Hon Mune Gatame. Figures 157 to 167 show Ray throwing Uke with Harai Goshi from the front. Figures 168 and 169 show Ray moving from Harai Goshi into Hon Mune Gatame from the front. Figure 170 shows Ray pinning Uke with Hon Mune Gatame from the front.

Fig. 161

Fig. 163

Fig. 162

Fig. 164

Fig. 165

Fig. 167

Fig. 166

Fig. 168 Transition from Harai Goshi to Hon Mune Gatame from the front.

Fig. 169

Fig. 171 Harai Goshi from the back.

Fig. 170 Hon Mune Gatame from the front.

Figures 171 to 180 show Ray throwing Uke with Harai Goshi from the back. Figures 181 to 185 show Ray moving from Harai Goshi into Hon Mune Gatame from the back. Figure 186 shows Ray pinning Uke with Hon Mune Gatame from the back.

Fig. 172

Fig. 173

Fig. 174

Fig. 175

Fig. 176

Fig. 177

Fig. 179

Fig. 178

Fig. 180

Fig. 181 Transition from Harai Goshi to Hon Mune Gatame from the back.

Fig. 183

Fig. 182

Fig. 184

Fig. 185

Fig. 186 Hon Mune Gatame from the back.

Sequence Six

Figures 187 to 216 show Ray throwing Uke with Ippon Seoi Nage and pinning Uke to the floor with Kuzure Mune Gatame. Figures 187 to 198 show Ray throwing Uke with Ippon Seoi Nage from the front. Figures 199 to 201 show Ray moving from Ippon Seoi Nage into Kuzure Mune Gatame from the front. Figures 202 and 203 show Ray pinning Uke with Kuzure Mune Gatame from the front.

Fig. 187 Ippon Seoi Nage from the front.

Fig. 188

Fig. 189

Fig. 190

Fig. 191

Fig. 192

Fig. 194

Fig. 193

Fig. 195

Fig. 196

Fig. 198

Fig. 197

Fig. 199 Transition from Ippon Seoi Nage to Kuzure Mune Gatame from the front.

Fig. 200

Fig. 202 Kuzure Mune Gatame from the front.

Fig. 201

Fig. 203

Figures 204 to 214 show Ray throwing Uke with Ippon Seoi Nage from the back. Figure 215 shows Ray moving from Ippon Seoi Nage into Kuzure Mune Gatame from the back. Figure 216 shows Ray pinning Uke with Kuzure Mune Gatame from the back.

Fig. 205

Fig. 204 Ippon Seoi Nage from the back.

Fig. 206

Fig. 207

Fig. 209

Fig. 208

Fig. 210

Fig. 211

Fig. 212

Fig. 213

Fig. 214

Fig. 215 Transition from Ippon Seoi Nage to Kuzure Mune Gatame from the back.

Fig. 216 Kuzure Mune Gatame from the back.

Sequence Seven

Figures 217 to 254 show Ray throwing Uke with O Uchi Gari and pinning Uke to the floor with Kuzure Yoko Shiho Gatame. Figures 217 to 226 show Ray throwing Uke with O Uchi Gari from the front. Figures 227 to 230 show Ray moving from O Uchi Gari into Kuzure Yoko Shiho Gatame from the front. Figures 231 and 232 show Ray pinning Uke with Kuzure Yoko Shiho Gatame from the front.

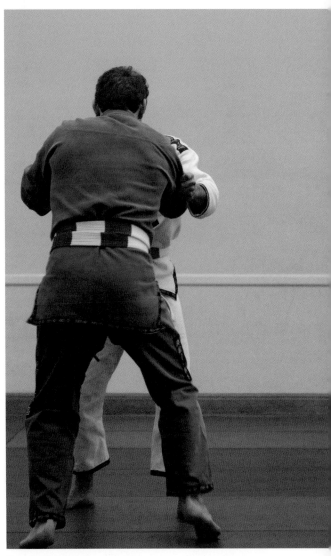

Fig. 217 O Uchi Gari from the front.

Fig. 218

Fig. 219

Fig. 220

Fig. 221

Fig. 222

Fig. 224

Fig. 223

Fig. 225

Fig. 226

Fig. 228

Fig. 227 Transition from O Uchi Gari to Kuzure Yoko Shiho Gatame from the front.

Fig. 229

Fig. 232

Figures 233 to 243 show Ray throwing Uke with O Uchi Gari from the back. Figures 244 to 252 show Ray moving from O Uchi Gari into Kuzure Yoko Shiho Gatame from the back. Figures 253 and 254 show Ray pinning Uke with Kuzure Yoko Shiho Gatame from the back.

Fig. 230

Fig. 231 Kuzure Yoko Shiho Gatame from the front.

Fig. 233 O Uchi Gari from the back.

Fig. 234

Fig. 235

Fig. 236

Fig. 237

Fig. 238

Fig. 240

Fig. 239

Fig. 241

Fig. 242

Fig. 243

Fig. 244 Transition from O Uchi Gari to Kuzure Yoko Shiho Gatame from the back.

Fig. 245

Fig. 246

Fig. 248

Fig. 247

Fig. 249

Fig. 250

Fig. 252

Fig. 251

Fig. 253 Kuzure Yoko Shiho Gatame from the back.

Fig. 254

INDEX

RELATED TITLES FROM CROWOOD

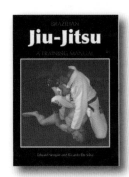

Brazilian Jiu-Jitsu
A Training Manual

EDWARD SEMPLE and
RICARDO DA SILVA

ISBN 978 1 86126 759 7
144pp, 250 illustrations

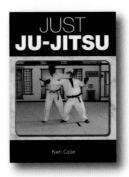

Just Ju-Jitsu

KEN COLE

ISBN 978 1 86126 849 5
224pp, 660 illustrations

The Essence of Jeet Kune Do

DAVE CARNELL

ISBN 978 1 84797 220 0
160pp, 395 illustrations

Ninjutsu

SIMON YEO

ISBN 978 1 86126 938 6
112pp, 150 illustrations

Jeet Kune Do
A Core Structure Training Manual

DAVE CARNELL

ISBN 978 1 84797 003 9
160pp, 350 illustrations

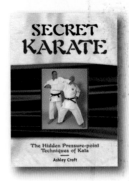

Secret Karate

ASHLEY CROFT

ISBN 978 1 86126 595 1
176pp, 330 illustrations

In case of difficulty ordering, contact the Sales Office:

The Crowood Press
Ramsbury
Wiltshire
SN8 2HR
UK

Tel: 44 (0) 1672 520320
enquiries@crowood.com

www.crowood.com